Thank you for learning
Korean with
Talk To Me In Korean!

(Kyeong-eun Choi (최경은))

Hyunwoo Sun

Cassie Casper

일상 속 진짜 자연스러운 **한국어 대화**
초급

Real-Life
Korean Conversations
For Beginners

written by TalkToMeInKorean

Real-Life Korean Conversations For Beginners

1판 1쇄	1st edition published	2017. 7. 17
1판 3쇄	3rd edition published	2018. 2. 20
지은이	Written by	TalkToMeInKorean
책임편집	Edited by	선경화 Kyung-hwa Sun, 스테파니 베이츠 Stephanie Bates, 에밀리 프리즈러키 Emily Przylucki
디자인	Designed by	선윤아 Yoona Sun
삽화	Illustrations by	까나리 존스 Kanari Jones
녹음	Voice Recordings by	TalkToMeInKorean
펴낸곳	Published by	롱테일북스 Longtail Books
펴낸이	Publisher	이수영 Su Young Lee
편집	Copy-edited by	김보경 Florence Kim
주소	Address	04043 서울 마포구 양화로 12길 16-9(서교동) 북앤빌딩 3층
		3rd Floor Book-And Bldg. 16-9 Yanghwa-ro 12-gil, Mapo-gu, Seoul, KOREA
전화	Telephone	+82-2-3144-2708
팩스	Fax	+82-2-3144-2597
이메일	E-mail	TTMIK@longtailbooks.co.kr
ISBN	979-11-86701-62-1	13710

*이 교재의 내용을 사전 허가 없이 전재하거나 복제할 경우 법적인 제재를 받게 됨을 알려 드립니다.

*잘못된 책은 구입하신 서점이나 본사에서 교환해 드립니다.

*정가는 표지에 표시되어 있습니다.

Real-Life Korean Conversations For Beginners

일상 속 진짜 자연스러운 **한국어 대화 초급**

Table of Contents

Preface

One of the best ways to learn a new language is to expose yourself to normal conversations between native speakers. This can be done by listening to native speakers talk, listening to a recording of people talking, or by reading dialogues that have been written to match the learner's level.

This book contains 40 different topics that have two sets of dialogues each - one is very simple and easy, while the other one is longer and more complex. They are all common situations that you may experience in day-to-day life. You can listen to every word and sentence in the book using the accompanying audio tracks, and then you can study the vocabulary words and grammar points used in each situation. Every chapter also includes a cultural tip that will help you better understand Korean life.

What more can we say? You have chosen a great book to help you improve your reading comprehension and speaking skills, so let's jump right in! You can study the dialogues from first to last, or choose any topic that interests you and learn the dialogues that way. Thank you for choosing to study with us and be sure to check out our other books and lessons on our website at TalkToMeInKorean.com!

How to Use This Book

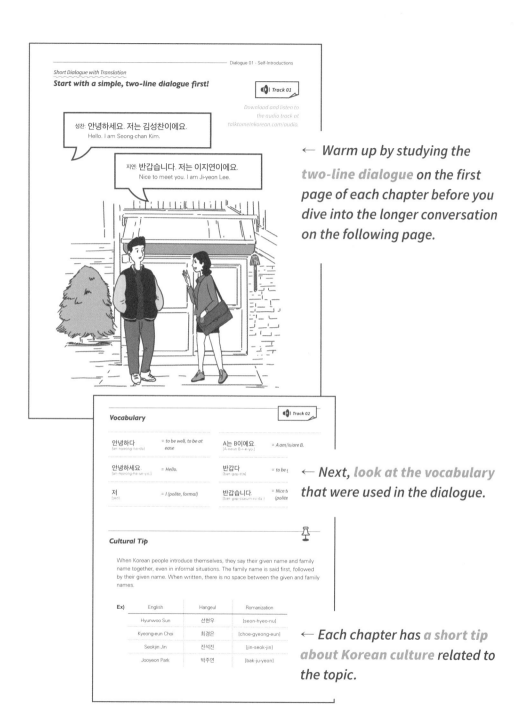

Short Dialogue with Translation

Start with a simple, two-line dialogue first!

🔊 **Track 01**

Download and listen to
the audio track at
talktomeinkorean.com/audio.

성찬: 안녕하세요. 저는 김성찬이에요.
Hello. I am Seong-chan Kim.

지연: 반갑습니다. 저는 이지연이에요.
Nice to meet you. I am Ji-yeon Lee.

← *Warm up by studying the*
two-line dialogue *on the first
page of each chapter before you
dive into the longer conversation
on the following page.*

Vocabulary

🔊 **Track 02**

안녕하다 [an-nyeong-ha-da]	= to be well, to be at ease	A는 B이에요. [A-neun B-i-e-yo.]	= A am/is/are B.
안녕하세요. [an-nyeong-ha-se-yo.]	= Hello.	반갑다 [ban-gap-tta]	= to be g
저 [jeo]	= I (polite, formal)	반갑습니다. [ban-gap-sseum-ni-da.]	= Nice to (polite

← *Next,* ***look at the vocabulary***
that were used in the dialogue.

Cultural Tip

When Korean people introduce themselves, they say their given name and family name together, even in informal situations. The family name is said first, followed by their given name. When written, there is no space between the given and family names.

Ex)

English	Hangeul	Romanization
Hyunwoo Sun	선현우	[seon-hyeo-nu]
Kyeong-eun Choi	최경은	[choe-gyeong-eun]
Seokjin Jin	진석진	[jin-seok-jin]
Jooyeon Park	박주연	[bak-ju-yeon]

← *Each chapter has* ***a short tip
about Korean culture*** *related to
the topic.*

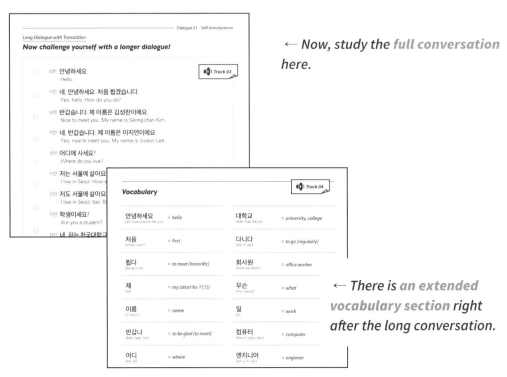

*← Now, study the **full conversation** here.*

*← **There is an extended vocabulary section** right after the long conversation.*

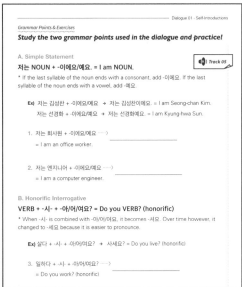

*← In the "**Grammar Points & Exercises**" section, study and practice the two grammar points that were used in the dialogue.*

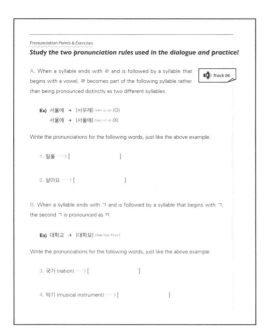

← In the "Pronunciation Points & Exercises" section, learn, practice, and review two pronunciation rules and patterns that were used in the dialogue.

← Some words will have a translation in parentheses. Other words will not have a translation because the meaning depends on the context of the sentence.

← On the last page of each chapter, read the short dialogue and the long conversation in Korean without any English translation.

Dialogue 01

반갑습니다
Nice to meet you.

•

Self-Introductions

Short Dialogue with Translation

Start with a simple, two-line dialogue first!

Download and listen to the audio track at talktomeinkorean.com/audio.

성찬: **안녕하세요. 저는 김성찬이에요.**
Hello. I am Seong-chan Kim.

지연: **반갑습니다. 저는 이지연이에요.**
Nice to meet you. I am Ji-yeon Lee.

Vocabulary

안녕하다 [an-nyeong-ha-da]	= *to be well, to be at ease*
안녕하세요. [an-nyeong-ha-se-yo.]	= *Hello.*
저 [jeo]	= *I (polite, formal)*
A은/는 B이에요/예요. [A-eun/neun B-i-e-yo/ye-yo.]	= *A am/is/are B.*
반갑다 [ban-gap-tta]	= *to be glad (to meet)*
반갑습니다. [ban-gap-sseum-ni-da.]	= *Nice to meet you. (polite, formal)*

Cultural Tip

When Korean people introduce themselves, they say their given name and family name together, even in informal situations. The family name is said first, followed by their given name. When written, there is no space between the given and family names.

Ex)

English	Hangeul	Romanization
Hyunwoo Sun	선현우	[seon-hyeo-nu]
Kyeong-eun Choi	최경은	[choe-gyeong-eun]
Seokjin Jin	진석진	[jin-seok-jin]
Jooyeon Park	박주연	[bak-ju-yeon]

Long Dialogue with Translation
Now challenge yourself with a longer dialogue!

◀)) *Track 03*

성찬: **안녕하세요.**
Hello.

지연: **네, 안녕하세요. 처음 뵙겠습니다.**
Yes, hello. How do you do?

성찬: **반갑습니다. 제 이름은 김성찬이에요.**
Nice to meet you. My name is Seong-chan Kim.

지연: **네, 반갑습니다. 제 이름은 이지연이에요.**
Yes, nice to meet you. My name is Ji-yeon Lee.

성찬: **어디에 사세요?**
Where do you live?

지연: **저는 서울에 살아요. 성찬 씨는요?**
I live in Seoul. How about you, Seong-chan?

성찬: **저도 서울에 살아요. 그런데 고향은 부산이에요.**
I live in Seoul, too. But, my hometown is Busan.

지연: **학생이세요?**
Are you a student?

성찬: **네. 저는 한국대학교에 다녀요. 지연 씨도 학생이세요?**
Yes, I go to Hanguk University. Ji-yeon, are you also a student?

지연: **아니요, 저는 회사원이에요.**
No, I am an office worker.

성찬: **무슨 일을 하세요?**
What kind of work do you do?

지연: **저는 컴퓨터 엔지니어예요.**
I am a computer engineer.

Vocabulary

안녕하세요
[an-nyeong-ha-se-yo] = *hello*

처음
[cheo-eum] = *first*

뵙다
[boep-tta] = *to meet (honorific)*

제
[je] = *my (short for 저의)*

이름
[i-reum] = *name*

반갑다
[ban-gap-tta] = *to be glad (to meet)*

어디
[eo-di] = *where*

살다
[sal-da] = *to live*

그런데
[geu-reon-de] = *but, however*

고향
[go-hyang] = *hometown*

학생
[hak-ssaeng] = *student*

대학교
[dae-hak-kkyo] = *university, college*

다니다
[da-ni-da] = *to go (regularly)*

회사원
[hoe-sa-won] = *office worker*

무슨
[mu-seun] = *what*

일
[il] = *work*

컴퓨터
[keom-pyu-teo] = *computer*

엔지니어
[en-ji-ni-eo] = *engineer*

Grammar Points & Exercises

Study the two grammar points used in the dialogue and practice!

A. Simple Statement

저는 NOUN + -이에요/예요. = I am NOUN.

* If the last syllable of the noun ends with a consonant, add -이에요. If the last syllable of the noun ends with a vowel, add -예요.

> **Ex)** 저는 김성찬 + -이에요/예요 → 저는 김성찬이에요. = I am Seong-chan Kim.
>
> 저는 선경화 + -이에요/예요 → 저는 선경화예요. = I am Kyung-hwa Sun.

> 1. 저는 회사원 + -이에요/예요 ······⟩ _____
>
>   = I am an office worker.

> 2. 저는 엔지니어 + -이에요/예요 ······⟩ _____
>
>   = I am a computer engineer.

B. Honorific Interrogative

VERB + -시- + -아/어/여요? = Do you VERB? (honorific)

* When -시- is combined with -아/어/여요, it becomes -셔요. Over time however, it changed to -세요 because it is easier to pronounce.

> **Ex)** 살다 + -시- + -아/어/여요? → 사세요? = Do you live? (honorific)

> 3. 일하다 + -시- + -아/어/여요? ······⟩ _____
>
>   = Do you work? (honorific)

> 4. 가르치다 + -시- + -아/어/여요? ······⟩ _____
>
>   = Do you teach? (honorific)

Study the two pronunciation rules used in the dialogue and practice!

A. When a syllable ends with ㄹ and is followed by a syllable that begins with a vowel, ㄹ becomes part of the following syllable rather than being pronounced distinctly as two different syllables.

Track 06

> **Ex)** 서울에 → [서우레] [seo-u-re] (O)
>
> 　　 서울에 → [서울에] [seo-ul-e] (X)

Write the pronunciations for the following words, just like the above example.

　1. 일을 ······> [　　　　　　　　　]

　2. 살아요 ······> [　　　　　　　　　]

B. When a syllable ends with ㄱ and is followed by a syllable that begins with ㄱ, the second ㄱ is pronounced as ㄲ.

> **Ex)** 대학교 → [대학꾜] [dae-hak-kkyo]

Write the pronunciations for the following words, just like the above example.

　3. 국가 (nation) ······> [　　　　　　　　　]

　4. 악기 (musical instrument) ······> [　　　　　　　　　]

Can you understand the entire dialogue without a translation? Test yourself!

Short Dialogue

성찬: 안녕하세요. 저는 김성찬이에요.

지연: 반갑습니다. 저는 이지연이에요.

Long Dialogue

성찬: 안녕하세요.

지연: 네, 안녕하세요. 처음 뵙겠습니다.

성찬: 반갑습니다. 제 이름은 김성찬이에요.

지연: 네, 반갑습니다. 제 이름은 이지연이에요.

성찬: 어디에 사세요?

지연: 저는 서울에 살아요. 성찬 씨는요?

성찬: 저도 서울에 살아요. 그런데 고향은 부산이에요.

지연: 학생이세요?

성찬: 네. 저는 한국대학교에 다녀요. 지연 씨도 학생이세요?

지연: 아니요, 저는 회사원이에요.

성찬: 무슨 일을 하세요?

지연: 저는 컴퓨터 엔지니어예요.

Answer Key for grammar exercises

1. 저는 회사원이에요. *2.* 저는 엔지니어예요. *3.* 일하세요? *4.* 가르치세요?

Answer Key for pronunciation exercises

1. 이를 *2.* 사라요 *3.* 국까 *4.* 악끼

제 명함이에요.

Here is my business card.

·

Exchanging Numbers

Short Dialogue with Translation

Start with a simple, two-line dialogue first!

 Track 07

수철: **연락처 좀 알려 주세요.**
Please let me know your contact information.

미영: **여기요. 제 명함이에요.**
Here. This is my business card.

Vocabulary

연락처
[yeol-lak-cheo]

= contact information

좀
[jom]

= a little (often used as a filler without any meaning, such as the English "well", "um", or "hm")

알리다
[al-li-da]

= to let (someone) know, to inform

VERB + -아/어/여 주다
[-a/eo/yeo ju-da]

= to VERB (for someone)

여기
[yeo-gi]

= here

제
[je]

= my (short for 저의)

명함
[myeong-ham]

= business card

NOUN + -이에요/예요
[-i-e-yo/ye-yo]

= to be + NOUN

Cultural Tip

The standard Korean word for "mobile phone" was 휴대폰 [hyu-dae-pon] until the term 핸드폰 [haen-deu-pon] (lit. hand phone) became more popular. It is now used on a daily basis. Both terms are recognized as standard Korean words, so therefore can be found in the dictionary. Young Korean speakers generally refer to mobile phones as 폰 [pon] (lit. phone). 스마트폰 [seu-ma-teu-pon] (lit. smartphone) is rarely used unless to differentiate between a regular non-smartphone mobile device and a smartphone.

Long Dialogue with Translation

Now challenge yourself with a longer dialogue!

🔊) *Track 09*

수철: **오늘 반가웠습니다.**
It was nice to meet you today.

미영: **네, 저도 만나서 반가웠어요.**
Yes, I was glad to meet you as well.

수철: **다시 만나고 싶어요.**
I want to meet you again.

미영: **네, 저도요.**
Yes, me too.

수철: **연락처 좀 알려 주세요.**
Please let me know your contact information.

미영: **여기요. 제 명함이에요.**
Here. This is my business card.

수철: **감사합니다. 저는 아직 명함이 없어요. 제 핸드폰 번호 알려 드릴게요.**
Thank you. I don't have a business card yet. I will give you my phone number.

미영: **그럼 제 번호로 전화해 주세요.**
Then, call me at my number.

수철: **네. 지금 전화하고 있어요.**
Yes, I'm calling you now.

미영: **전화 왔어요.**
I got the call.

수철: **그게 제 번호예요. 저장해 주세요.**
That's my number. Please save it.

미영: **네. 그럼 다음에 또 봐요.**
Yes. Well, I will see you next time.

Vocabulary

오늘
[o-neul]
= today

번호
[beo-no]
= number

반갑다
[ban-gap-tta]
= to be glad (to meet)

알려 드리다
[al-lyeo deu-ri-da]
= to let (someone) know (honorific)

만나다
[man-na-da]
= to meet

전화하다
[jeo-nwa-ha-da]
= to call

연락처
[yeol-lak-cheo]
= contact information

오다
[o-da]
= to come

알려 주다
[al-lyeo ju-da]
= to let (someone) know

저장하다
[jeo-jang-ha-da]
= to save

여기
[yeo-gi]
= here

다음
[da-eum]
= next

명함
[myeong-ham]
= business card

뵙다
[boep-tta]
= to see, to meet (honorific)

감사하다
[gam-sa-ha-da]
= to be thankful

아직
[a-jik]
= yet

없다
[eop-tta]
= to not exist, to not have, to not be there

핸드폰
[haen-deu-pon]
= cell phone

Grammar Points & Exercises

Study the two grammar points used in the dialogue and practice!

A. Polite Request

VERB + -아/어/여 주세요. = Please VERB (me).

) Track 11

* If the verb stem ends with ㅏ or ㅗ, it is followed by -아 주세요. If the verb stem ends with 하, it is followed by -여 주세요. For all other verb stem endings, use -어 주세요.

Ex)

전화하다 + -아/어/여 주세요 → 전화하여 주세요. → 전화해 주세요. = Please call (me).

만나다 + -아/어/여 주세요 → 만나아 주세요. → 만나 주세요. = Please meet (me).

가르치다 + -아/어/여 주세요 → 가르치어 주세요. → 가르쳐 주세요. = Please teach (me).

1. 저장하다 + -아/어/여 주세요 ······⟩ _____ = Please save (it).

2. 알리다 + -아/어/여 주세요 ······⟩ _____ = Please let (me) know.

B. Present Progressive

VERB +-고 있어요. = I am VERB-ing.

Ex) 전화하다 + -고 있어요 → 전화하고 있어요. = I'm calling now.

3. 만나다 + -고 있어요 ······⟩ _____ = I'm meeting now.

4. 저장하다 + -고 있어요 ······⟩ _____ = I'm saving (it) now.

Study the two pronunciation rules used in the dialogue and practice!

A. When a syllable ends with ㄴ and is followed by a syllable that begins with ㄹ, the ㄴ is pronounced as ㄹ.

Ex) 연락처 → [열락처]

Write the pronunciations for the following words, just like the above example.

1. 난로 (heater, stove) ······> [   ]

2. 분리하다 (to separate) ······> [   ]

B. When a syllable ends with ㅂ and is followed by a syllable that begins with ㄴ, the ㅂ is pronounced as ㅁ.

Ex) 감사합니다 → [감사함니다]

Write the pronunciations for the following words, just like the above example.

3. 잡는 ······> [   ]

4. 갑니다 ······> [   ]

Korean Only

Can you understand the entire dialogue without a translation? Test yourself!

- *Short Dialogue*

수철: 연락처 좀 알려 주세요.

미영: 여기요. 제 명함이에요.

- *Long Dialogue*

수철: 오늘 반가웠습니다.

미영: 네, 저도 만나서 반가웠어요.

수철: 다시 만나고 싶어요.

미영: 네, 저도요.

수철: 연락처 좀 알려 주세요.

미영: 여기요. 제 명함이에요.

수철: 감사합니다. 저는 아직 명함이 없어요. 제 핸드폰 번호 알려
　　 드릴게요.

미영: 그럼 제 번호로 전화해 주세요.

수철: 네. 지금 전화하고 있어요.

미영: 전화 왔어요.

수철: 그게 제 번호예요. 저장해 주세요.

미영: 네. 그럼 다음에 또 봐요.

Answer Key for grammar exercises

1. 저장해 주세요. *2.* 알려 주세요. *3.* 만나고 있어요. *4.* 저장하고 있어요.

Answer Key for pronunciation exercises

1. 날로 *2.* 불리하다 *3.* 잠는 *4.* 감니다

잘 지내고 있어?
How are you doing?

•

How are you?

Short Dialogue with Translation
Start with a simple, two-line dialogue first!

 Track 13

수경: **지민아, 잘 지내고 있어?**
Jimin, how are you doing?

지민: **응. 잘 지내. 너는 어때?**
Yeah. I'm doing well. How about you?

Vocabulary

잘 [jal]	= well
지내다 [ji-nae-da]	= to live, to stay, to spend (time)
VERB + -고 있다 [-go it-tta]	= to be + VERB-ing
응 [eung]	= yes, yeah, ok (casual)
너 [neo]	= you
NOUN + 어때? [eo-ttae]	= How is/are + NOUN? (casual)

Cultural Tip

In Korea, people will usually announce their wedding date about a month before the event. Around that time, they will mail out wedding invitations to relatives and friends who live far away, but will meet up with close friends to hand out the invitations in person.

Long Dialogue with Translation
Now challenge yourself with a longer dialogue!

수경: **여보세요?**
Hello?

지민: **여보세요? 수경아, 나야!**
Hello? Su-gyeong, it's me!

수경: **누구세요?**
Who is this?

지민: **나 지민이! 잘 지내고 있어?**
It's me, Ji-min. How are you doing?

수경: **응, 지민아. 나는 잘 지내. 너는 어때?**
Yeah, Ji-min. I am doing well. How about you?

지민: **나도 잘 지내. 나 곧 결혼해. 그래서 요즘 너무 바빠.**
I am doing well, too. I am getting married soon. So, I'm really busy these days.

수경: **정말? 축하해.**
Really? Congratulations!

지민: **고마워.**
Thank you.

수경: **언제 결혼해?**
When are you getting married?

지민: **다음 달에 해. 주연이하고 같이 와.**
I'm getting married next month. Please come with Joo-yeon.

수경: **응. 알겠어.**
Ok. I got it.

지민: **그럼 그때 보자. 끊을게.**
Well, I'll see you then. I gotta go.

수경: **응. 그래. 그때 봐.**
Yeah, ok. See you then.

Vocabulary

여보세요? [yeo-bo-se-yo?]	= Hello? (on the phone)	축하하다 [chu-ka-ha-da]	= to congratulate, to celebrate
누구 [nu-gu]	= who	고맙다 [go-map-tta]	= to be thankful
잘 [jal]	= well	언제 [eon-je]	= when
지내다 [ji-nae-da]	= to live, to stay, to spend (time)	다음 [da-eum]	= next
곧 [got]	= soon	달 [dal]	= month
결혼하다 [gyeo-ro-na-da]	= to get married	같이 [ga-chi]	= together
그래서 [geu-rae-seo]	= so, therefore	오다 [o-da]	= to come
요즘 [yo-jeum]	= these days	그럼 [geu-reom]	= then
너무 [neo-mu]	= really, so, too much	그때 [geu-ttae]	= then, at that time
바쁘다 [ba-ppeu-da]	= to be busy	보다 [bo-da]	= to see, to watch
정말 [jeong-mal]	= really, very	끊다 [kkeun-ta]	= to hang up

Grammar Points & Exercises

Study the two grammar points used in the dialogue and practice!

A. Imperative Form

VERB + -자 = Let's VERB. (casual)

Ex) 보다 + -자 → 보자. = Let's see.

1. 결혼하다 + -자 ……〉 _____ = Let's get married.

2. 끊다 + -자 ……〉 _____ = Let's hang up.

B. Simple Future Tense

VERB + -(으)ㄹ게(요) = I will VERB

* Unless you are speaking to someone very close to you, you should end the sentence with -요 to be polite.

Ex) 끊다 + -(으)ㄹ게(요) → 끊을게(요). = I will hang up.

3. 오다 + -(으)ㄹ게(요) ……〉 _____ = I will come.

4. 보다 + -(으)ㄹ게(요) ……〉 _____ = I will see.

Study the two pronunciation rules used in the dialogue and practice!

A. When a syllable ends with ㄹ and is followed by a syllable that begins with ㅎ, ㄹ becomes part of the following syllable and ㅎ is dropped.

*Not an official pronunciation rule, but it is done for easier pronunciation.

Ex) 결혼 → [겨론]

Write the pronunciations for the following words, just like the above example.

1. 잘하다 (to be good at) ······> [   ]

2. 일하다 (to work) ······> [   ]

B. When a syllable ends with ㄱ and is followed by a syllable that begins with ㅎ, ㄱ becomes part of the following syllable and is pronounced as ㅋ.

Ex) 축하하다 → [추카하다]

Write the pronunciations for the following words, just like the above example.

3. 독하다 (to be potent, to be spiteful) ······> [   ]

4. 시작하다 (to start) ······> [   ]

Korean Only

Can you understand the entire dialogue without a translation? Test yourself!

- *Short Dialogue*

수경: 지민아, 잘 지내고 있어?

지민: 응. 잘 지내. 너는 어때?

- *Long Dialogue*

수경: 여보세요?

지민: 여보세요? 수경아, 나야!

수경: 누구세요?

지민: 나 지민이! 잘 지내고 있어?

수경: 응, 지민아. 나는 잘 지내. 너는 어때?

지민: 나도 잘 지내. 나 곧 결혼해. 그래서 요즘 너무 바빠.

수경: 정말? 축하해.

지민: 고마워.

수경: 언제 결혼해?

지민: 다음 달에 해. 주연이하고 같이 와.

수경: 응. 알겠어.

지민: 그럼 그때 보자. 끊을게.

수경: 응. 그래. 그때 봐.

Answer Key for grammar exercises

1. 결혼하자. *2.* 끊자. *3.* 올게(요). *4.* 볼게(요).

Answer Key for pronunciation exercises

1. 자라다 *2.* 이라다 *3.* 도카다 *4.* 시자카다

이번 주 토요일에 뭐 해?

What are you doing this Saturday?

•

Plans

Short Dialogue with Translation

Start with a simple, two-line dialogue first!

 Track 19

소영: **민우야, 우리 영화 보러 가자.**
Min-woo, let's go see a movie.

민우: **그래. 좋아.**
Ok. Good.

Vocabulary

우리 [u-ri]	= *we*
영화 [yeong-hwa]	= *movie*
보다 [bo-da]	= *to see, to watch*
VERB + **-(으)러 가다** [-(eu-)reo ga-da]	= *to go to VERB*
VERB + **-자** [-ja]	= *let's VERB (casual)*
그래 [geu-rae]	= *ok (casual)*
좋다 [jo-ta]	= *to be good, to like*

Cultural Tip

When addressing someone using **반말** (casual language), the speaker will typically add -아 or -야 to the end of the name. Names that end in a vowel are followed by -야, and names that end in a consonant are followed by -아.

Ex)

경은 → 경은아! [gyeong-eu-na!] = Hey, Kyeong-eun!

현우 → 현우야! [hyeo-nu-ya!] = Hey, Hyunwoo!

Long Dialogue with Translation
Now challenge yourself with a longer dialogue!

◀)) *Track 21*

소영: **민우야, 이번 주 토요일에 뭐 해?**
Min-woo, what are you doing this Saturday?

민우: **토요일? 토요일에 친구 생일이라서 친구 만날 거야.**
Saturday? It's my friend's birthday on Saturday, so I'm meeting my friend.

소영: **그럼 일요일은?**
How about Sunday?

민우: **일요일은 아직 아무 계획 없어. 왜?**
I don't have any plans for Sunday. Why?

소영: **그럼 일요일에 우리 만나자.**
Then let's meet on Sunday.

민우: **왜? 무슨 일 있어?**
Why? Anything happening?

소영: **아니. 아무 일도 없어. 그냥 보고 싶어서.**
No. Nothing happening. I just wanted to see you.

민우: **지금 데이트 신청하는 거야?**
Are you asking me out on a date now?

소영: **응. 맞아. 우리 영화 보러 가자.**
Yeah, that's right. Let's go see a movie.

민우: **그래. 좋아. 몇 시에 볼까?**
Ok. Good. What time shall we meet?

소영: **세 시에 영화관 앞에서 보자.**
Let's meet in front of the movie theater at 3.

민우: **알겠어.**
I got it.

Vocabulary

이번 [i-beon]	= this, this time	무슨 [mu-seun]	= what, something
주 [ju]	= week	일 [il]	= work
토요일 [to-yo-il]	= Saturday	있다 [it-tta]	= to exist, to have
뭐 [mwo]	= what, something	그냥 [geu-nyang]	= just, just because

* The dictionary form is 무엇, but people often just say 뭐 for ease of pronunciation.

		보고 싶다 [bo-go sip-tta]	= to miss
하다 [ha-da]	= to do	데이트 [de-i-teu]	= date
친구 [chin-gu]	= friend	신청하다 [sin-cheong-ha-da]	= to apply for
생일 [saeng-il]	= birthday	영화 [yeong-hwa]	= movie
만나다 [man-na-da]	= to meet, to see	보다 [bo-da]	= to see, to watch
일요일 [i-ryo-il]	= Sunday	가다 [ga-da]	= to go
아직 [a-jik]	= yet	좋다 [jo-ta]	= to be good, to like
아무 [a-mu]	= any	몇 시 [myeot si]	= what time
계획 [gye-hoek]	= plans	세 시 [se si]	= three o'clock
없다 [eop-tta]	= to not exist, to not have, to not be there	영화관 [yeong-hwa-gwan]	= movie theater
왜 [wae]	= why	앞 [ap]	= front
우리 [u-ri]	= we	알다 [al-da]	= to know

Grammar Points & Exercises

Study the two grammar points used in the dialogue and practice!

A. Subordinating Conjunction with a Noun

NOUN + -(이)라서 = because it is NOUN

🔊) *Track 23*

* If a noun ends with a vowel, attach -라서 at the end, and if it ends with a consonant, use -이라서.

> **Ex)** 생일 + -(이)라서 → 생일이라서 = because it is one's birthday
>
> 숙제 + -(이)라서 → 숙제라서 = because it is homework

> **1.** 토요일 + -(이)라서 ······〉   = because it is Saturday
> _____

> **2.** 세 시 + -(이)라서 ······〉   = because it is 3 o'clock
> _____

B. Subordinating Conjunction with a Verb/Adjective

VERB/ADJECTIVE + -아/어/여서

= because I VERB / because I am ADJECTIVE

* If the verb stem ends with ㅏ or ㅗ, it is followed by -아서. If the verb stem ends with 하, it is followed by -여서. For all other verb stem endings, use -어서.

> **Ex)** 가다 + -아/어/여서 → 가아서 → 가서 = because I go
>
> 보고 싶다 + -아/어/여서 → 보고 싶어서 = because I want to see
>
> 신청하다 + -아/어/여서 → 신청하여서 → 신청해서 = because I apply

> **3.** 바쁘다 + -아/어/여서 ······〉   = because I am busy
> _____

4. 없다 + -아/어/여서 ……> _____ = because I don't have

Study the two pronunciation rules used in the dialogue and practice!

A. When a syllable ends with -(으)ㄹ and is followed by a syllable that begins with ㄱ, the ㄱ is pronounced as ㄲ.

🔊) *Track 24*

Ex) 만날 거야 → [만날 꺼야]

Write the pronunciations for the following words, just like the above example.

1. 갈 거야 (I am going to go) ……> [   ]

2. 볼 거야 (I am going to see) ……> [   ]

B. When ㅊ is used as 받침, or a final consonant, it is pronounced like ㄷ.

Ex) 몇 → [면]

Write the pronunciations for the following words, just like the above example.

3. 꽃 (flower) ……> [   ]

4. 빛 (light) ……> [   ]

Korean Only

Can you understand the entire dialogue without a translation? Test yourself!

- Short Dialogue

소영: 민우야, 우리 영화 보러 가자.

민우: 그래. 좋아.

- Long Dialogue

소영: 민우야, 이번 주 토요일에 뭐 해?

민우: 토요일? 토요일에 친구 생일이라서 친구 만날 거야.

소영: 그럼 일요일은?

민우: 일요일은 아직 아무 계획 없어. 왜?

소영: 그럼 일요일에 우리 만나자.

민우: 왜? 무슨 일 있어?

소영: 아니. 아무 일도 없어. 그냥 보고 싶어서.

민우: 지금 데이트 신청하는 거야?

소영: 응. 맞아. 우리 영화 보러 가자.

민우: 그래. 좋아. 몇 시에 볼까?

소영: 세 시에 영화관 앞에서 보자.

민우: 알겠어.

Answer Key for grammar exercises

1. 토요일이라서 *2.* 세 시라서 *3.* 바빠서 *4.* 없어서

Answer Key for pronunciation exercises

1. 갈 꺼야 *2.* 볼 꺼야 *3.* 꼳 *4.* 빋

Dialogue 05

너도 와!
You should come, too!

•

Dinner

Short Dialogue with Translation
Start with a simple, two-line dialogue first!

Track 25

현우: 내일 어디로 가면 돼?
Where should I go tomorrow?

세경: 내일 퇴근 후에 나랑 같이 가자.
Let's go together after work tomorrow.

Vocabulary

내일 [nae-il]	= tomorrow		NOUN + 후에 [hu-e]	= after + NOUN
어디 [eo-di]	= where		나 [na]	= I, me (casual)
-(으)로 [-(eu)-ro]	= to, toward		-(이)랑 [-(i)-rang]	= with
가다 [ga-da]	= to go		같이 [ga-chi]	= together
퇴근 [toe-geun]	= getting off work		-자 [-ja]	= let's (casual)

VERB + -(으)면 되다
[-(eu)-myeon doe-da]

= to just have to + VERB, to be just supposed to + VERB, can just + VERB

Cultural Tip

When native Korean speakers suggest having a drink, they use the expression "한잔하다". When translated literally, 한 means "one", 잔 means "glass" (and is also used as a counter for alcohol), and 하다 means "to do" or "to have". Therefore, they say, "to have one glass" as a suggestion. Let's have a glass!

Long Dialogue with Translation

Now challenge yourself with a longer dialogue!

현우: **세경아, 내일 바빠?**
Se-kyeong, are you busy tomorrow?

세경: **내일 선영이 만나.**
I'm meeting Seon-yeong tomorrow.

현우: **그래?**
You are?

세경: **응. 왜? 무슨 일 있어?**
Yeah. Why? Anything happening?

현우: **아니, 그냥. 술 한잔하고 싶어서.**
No, nothing. I wanted to have a drink.

세경: **그래? 내일 우리도 술 한잔할 거야. 너도 와!**
Really? We are also going to have a drink tomorrow. You should come, too!

현우: **그래도 돼?**
Is it ok?

세경: **응, 와도 돼. 선영이도 괜찮을 거야.**
Yeah, you can come. I think Seon-yeong will be fine with that.

현우: **좋아. 그럼 어디로 가면 돼?**
Sounds good. Then, where should I go?

세경: **내일 퇴근 후에 나랑 같이 가자.**
Let's go together after work tomorrow.

현우: **선영이는?**
How about Seon-yeong?

세경: **선영이는 일곱 시까지 술집으로 올 거야.**
Seon-yeong will come to the pub by 7.

Track 27

Vocabulary

내일 [nae-il]	= tomorrow		**오다** [o-da]	= to come
바쁘다 [ba-ppeu-da]	= to be busy		**괜찮다** [gwaen-chan-ta]	= to be ok, to be alright
만나다 [man-na-da]	= to meet		**좋다** [jo-ta]	= to be good, to like
왜 [wae]	= why		**그럼** [geu-reom]	= then
무슨 [mu-seun]	= what		**어디** [eo-di]	= where
일 [il]	= work		**가다** [ga-da]	= to go
있다 [it-tta]	= to exist, to have		**퇴근** [toe-geun]	= getting off work
그냥 [geu-nyang]	= just, just because		**후** [hu]	= after
술 [sul]	= alcoholic drink		**같이** [ga-chi]	= together
우리 [u-ri]	= we		**일곱 시** [il-gop si]	= seven o'clock
한잔하다 [han-ja-na-da]	= to have a drink		**술집** [sul-jjip]	= pub, bar

Grammar Points & Exercises

Study the two grammar points used in the dialogue and practice!

A. Giving Permission

VERB + -아/어/여도 돼(요) = you can VERB / it is ok to VERB

Ex) 오다 + -아/어/여도 돼(요). → 와도 돼(요).

= You can come. / It is ok for you to come.

1. 한잔하다 + -아/어/여도 돼(요) ……〉 _____

= You can have a drink. / It is ok for you to have a drink.

2. 가다 + -아/어/여도 돼(요) ……〉 _____

= You can go/leave. / It is ok for you to leave.

B. Asking about the Requirements/Instructions When Given a Task

VERB + -(으)면 돼(요)? : I just have to VERB? / So, all I have to do is VERB? / Is it ok if I just VERB?

* If a verb stem ends with a vowel, attach -면 돼(요)? at the end, and if it ends with a consonant, use -으면 돼(요)?

** There is no set translation of this phrase as the English meaning changes depending on the context of the sentence.

Ex) 가다 + -(으)면 돼(요)? → 가면 돼(요)? = I just have to go?

3. 만나다 + -(으)면 돼(요)? ……〉 _____

= So, all I have to do is meet?

4. 하다 + -(으)면 돼(요)? ······> _____

= Is it ok if I just do (it)?

Study the two pronunciation rules used in the dialogue and practice!

A. When a syllable ends with ㄶ and is followed by a syllable that begins with a vowel, only the ㄴ is pronounced, while the ㅎ is not pronounced.

Ex) 괜찮을 거야 → [괜찬을 꺼야]

* If you are wondering why 거야 has become 꺼야, please refer to page 42.

B. When a syllable ends with ㄴ and is followed by a syllable that begins with a vowel, ㄴ becomes part of the following syllable rather than being pronounced distinctly as two different syllables.

Ex) [괜찬을 꺼야] → [괜차늘 꺼야]

Write the pronunciations for the following words, just like the above example.

1. 많은 (a lot of) ······> [   ]

2. 끊을게 (I'll hang up) ······> [   ]

Korean Only

Can you understand the entire dialogue without a translation? Test yourself!

- Short Dialogue

현우: 내일 어디로 가면 돼?

세경: 내일 퇴근 후에 나랑 같이 가자.

- Long Dialogue

현우: 세경아, 내일 바빠?

세경: 내일 선영이 만나.

현우: 그래?

세경: 응. 왜? 무슨 일 있어?

현우: 아니, 그냥. 술 한잔하고 싶어서.

세경: 그래? 내일 우리도 술 한잔할 거야. 너도 와!

현우: 그래도 돼?

세경: 응, 와도 돼. 선영이도 괜찮을 거야.

현우: 좋아. 그럼 어디로 가면 돼?

세경: 내일 퇴근 후에 나랑 같이 가자.

현우: 선영이는?

세경: 선영이는 일곱 시까지 술집으로 올 거야.

Answer Key for grammar exercises

1. 한잔해도 돼(요). *2.* 가도 돼(요). *3.* 만나면 돼(요)? *4.* 하면 돼(요)?

Answer Key for pronunciation exercises

1. 마는 *2.* 끄늘께

Dialogue 06

결혼 축하해!
Congratulations on your wedding!

•

Wedding

Short Dialogue with Translation

Start with a simple, two-line dialogue first!

 Track 31

수정: **진영아, 결혼 정말 축하해!**
Jin-yeong, congratulations on your wedding!

진영: **고마워!**
Thank you!

Vocabulary

결혼
[gyeo-ron]

= *marriage, wedding*

정말
[jeong-mal]

= *really, very*

축하하다
[chu-ka-ha-da]

= *to congratulate, to celebrate*

고마워
[go-ma-wo]

= *Thank you (casual)*

Cultural Tip

In Korea, guests at a wedding usually give money as a gift to the couple. Guests can hand in their envelopes filled with cash at the reception desk of the wedding venue. If a guest would like to give a physical item, then they give it privately before or after the ceremony. However, most Korean couples leave for their honeymoon directly after the ceremony, so if you have a gift that is to be used while on honeymoon, you may give it to the couple at the wedding.

Long Dialogue with Translation

Now challenge yourself with a longer dialogue!

🔊) *Track 33*

수정: **진영아!**
Jin-yeong!

진영: **어! 수정아, 왔어?**
Oh, Su-jeong, you came?

수정: **응. 오늘 너무 예쁘다. 천사 같아. 결혼 정말 축하해!**
Yeah. You are so pretty today. You look like an angel.
Congratulations on your wedding!

진영: **고마워. 그런데 나 지금 너무 긴장돼.**
Thank you. But I'm really nervous right now.

수정: **정말? 긴장하지 마.**
Really? Don't be nervous.

진영: **응. 알겠어. 근데 혼자 왔어?**
Ok. I got it. But, did you come by yourself?

수정: **은진이는 오고 있어. 곧 도착할 거야.**
Eun-jin is on her way. She will arrive soon.

진영: **그렇구나.**
I see.

수정: **자, 결혼 선물이야.**
Here, it's a wedding present for you.

진영: **정말? 고마워. 이게 뭐야?**
Really? Thank you. What is it?

수정: **커플 티야. 신혼여행 가서 신랑하고 같이 입어.**
They are matching t-shirts. Wear them with your
husband on your honeymoon.

Vocabulary

오다 [o-da]	= to come	근데 [geun-de]	= but, however, by the way (short for 그런데)
오늘 [o-neul]	= today	곧 [got]	= soon
너무 [neo-mu]	= really, so, too much	도착하다 [do-cha-ka-da]	= to arrive
예쁘다 [ye-ppeu-da]	= to be pretty	선물 [seon-mul]	= gift
천사 [cheon-sa]	= angel	이것 [i-geot]	= this, this thing
결혼 [gyeo-ron]	= marriage, wedding	뭐 [mwo]	= what
정말 [jeong-mal]	= really, very	커플 티 [keo-peul ti]	= matching couple t-shirts
축하하다 [chu-ka-ha-da]	= to congratulate, to celebrate	신혼여행 [si-non-nyeo-haeng]	= honeymoon
고맙다 [go-map-tta]	= to be thankful	가다 [ga-da]	= to go
그런데 [geu-reon-de]	= but, however	신랑 [sil-lang]	= husband
지금 [ji-geum]	= now	같이 [ga-chi]	= together
긴장되다 [gin-jang-doe-da]	= to be nervous	입다 [ip-tta]	= to wear, to put on

Study the two grammar points used in the dialogue and practice!

A. Negative Present Tense

VERB + -지 마(요) = Don't VERB.

* If you want to be more polite, use VERB + -지 마세요.

> **Ex)** 긴장하다 + -지 마(요). → 긴장하지 마(요). = Don't be nervous.
>
> * 긴장하다 is a verb in Korean.

> **1.** 오다 + -지 마(요). ⋯⋯⟩ _____ = Don't come.

> **2.** 입다 + -지 마(요). ⋯⋯⟩ _____ = Don't wear (it).

B. Imperative Ending

VERB + -아/어/여(요). = (Do) VERB.

* This is the same form as plain present tense ending.

> **Ex)** 입다 + -아/어/여(요). → 입어(요). = Wear (it).

> **3.** 오다 + -아/어/여(요). ⋯⋯⟩ _____ = Come.

> **4.** 만나다 + -아/어/여(요). ⋯⋯⟩ _____ = Meet (me).

Study the two pronunciation rules used in the dialogue and practice!

A. When a syllable ends with ㅎ and is followed by a syllable that begins with ㄱ, the ㅎ changes the pronunciation of ㄱ to ㅋ. ㅎ is not pronounced because it is used to create the ㅋ sound.

Track 36

Ex) 그렇구나 → [그러쿠나]

Write the pronunciations for the following words, just like the above example.

1. 그렇게 (like that, as such) ······> [   ]

2. 파랗고 (blue and...) ······> [   ]

B. When it comes to compound words or derivatives, if the first word ends with a consonant and is followed by a word that begins with 여, ㄴ is added and pronounced as 녀.

Ex) 신혼여행 → [신혼녀행]

* 신혼여행 is a compound word: 신혼 meaning "new marriage" and 여행 meaning "travel".

Write the pronunciations for the following words, just like the above example.

3. 한여름 (midsummer) ······> [   ]

4. 맹장염 (appendicitis) ······> [   ]

Korean Only

Can you understand the entire dialogue without a translation? Test yourself!

- Short Dialogue

수정: 진영아, 결혼 정말 축하해!

진영: 고마워!

- Long Dialogue

수정: 진영아!

진영: 어! 수정아, 왔어?

수정: 응. 오늘 너무 예쁘다. 천사 같아. 결혼 정말 축하해!

진영: 고마워. 그런데 나 지금 너무 긴장돼.

수정: 정말? 긴장하지 마.

진영: 응. 알겠어. 근데 혼자 왔어?

수정: 은진이는 오고 있어. 곧 도착할 거야.

진영: 그렇구나.

수정: 자, 결혼 선물이야.

진영: 정말? 고마워. 이게 뭐야?

수정: 커플 티야. 신혼여행 가서 신랑하고 같이 입어.

Answer Key for grammar exercises

1. 오지 마(요). *2.* 입지 마(요). *3.* 와(요). *4.* 만나(요).

Answer Key for pronunciation exercises

1. 그러케 *2.* 파라코 *3.* 한녀름 *4.* 맹장념

오늘 집에 언제 들어와?

When are you coming home today?

Coming Home

Short Dialogue with Translation

Start with a simple, two-line dialogue first!

 Track 37

엄마: **오늘 집에 언제 들어와?**
When are you coming home today?

은비: **늦게 올 거예요.**
I will come home late.

Vocabulary

오늘
[o-neul]

= *today*

집
[jip]

= *house, home*

-에
[-e]

= *at, in, to (somewhere)*

언제
[eon-je]

= *when*

들어오다
[deu-reo-o-da]

= *to come in*

늦게
[neut-kke]

= *at a late hour*

* 늦게 is the adverb form of 늦다 (to be late).

오다
[o-da]

= *to come*

VERB + -(으)ㄹ 거예요.
[-(eu)l geo-ye-yo.]

= *I will VERB.*

Cultural Tip

In Korea, it is common for unmarried adults to live with their parents. If a person is not yet married and lives by themself, it is typically because their parents live far away from their office or school.

Long Dialogue with Translation

Now challenge yourself with a longer dialogue!

Track 39

엄마: **오늘 집에 언제 들어와? 늦어?**
When are you coming home today? Will you be late?

은비: **네. 늦게 올 거예요.**
Yes, I will come home late.

엄마: **어제보다 더 늦게 올 거야?**
Will you come home later than yesterday?

은비: **아직 몰라요.**
I don't know yet.

엄마: **저녁 먹고 올 거야?**
Will you come home after having dinner?

은비: **네. 먹고 올 거예요.**
Yes. I will eat (out) and come home.

엄마: **일이 많아?**
Do you have a lot of work?

은비: **네. 요즘 일이 많아서 바빠요.**
Yes. I have a lot of work these days, so I'm busy.

엄마: **그래도 저녁 꼭 먹어야 돼.**
But you need to make sure you have dinner.

은비: **네. 알겠어요.**
Yes, I will.

엄마: **12시 전에 와.**
Come home before midnight.

은비: **네. 노력해 볼게요.**
Yeah. I will try.

Vocabulary

오늘 [o-neul]	= today	오다 [o-da]	= to come
집 [jip]	= house, home	일 [il]	= work
언제 [eon-je]	= when	많다 [man-ta]	= to be a lot
들어오다 [deu-reo-o-da]	= to come in	요즘 [yo-jeum]	= these days
늦다 [neut-tta]	= to be late	바쁘다 [ba-ppeu-da]	= to be busy
어제 [eo-je]	= yesterday	그래도 [geu-rae-do]	= but, even so
-보다 [-bo-da]	= than	꼭 [kkok]	= make sure
더 [deo]	= more	알다 [al-da]	= to know, to understand
아직 [a-jik]	= yet	12시 [yeol-ttu si]	= 12 o'clock
모르다 [mo-reu-da]	= to not know	전 [jeon]	= before
저녁 [jeo-nyeok]	= dinner, evening	노력하다 [no-ryeo-ka-da]	= to try
먹다 [meok-tta]	= to eat		

Grammar Points & Exercises

Study the two grammar points used in the dialogue and practice!

A. Comparisons

◀)) *Track 41*

NOUN + -보다 더 = more than NOUN

Ex) 어제 + -보다 더 → 어제보다 더 = more than yesterday

1. 오늘 + -보다 더 ······⟩ _____ = more than today

2. 저녁 + -보다 더 ······⟩ _____ = more than dinner

B. Sequence

VERB + -고 오다 = to come after VERB-ing

Ex) 먹다 + -고 오다 → 먹고 오다 = to come after eating

3. 하다 + -고 오다 ······⟩ _____ = to come after doing

4. 만나다 + -고 오다 ······⟩ _____ = to come after meeting

Study the two pronunciation rules used in the dialogue and practice!

A. When ㅈ is used as 받침, or a final consonant, it is pronounced like ㄷ.

◀)) *Track 42*

Ex) 늦 → [늗]

Write the pronunciations for the following words, just like the above example.

1. 낮 (day, daytime) ······⟩ [   ]

2. 빚 (debt) ······⟩ [   ]

B. When a syllable ends with ㅈ (which sounds the same as ㄷ when in the 받침 position) and is followed by a syllable that begins with ㄱ, the ㄱ is pronounced as ㄲ.

Ex) 늦게 → [늗께]

Write the pronunciations for the following words, just like the above example.

3. 잊고 (forget and...) ······⟩ [   ]

4. 빚과 (debt and...) ······⟩ [   ]

Korean Only

Can you understand the entire dialogue without a translation? Test yourself!

- Short Dialogue

엄마: 오늘 집에 언제 들어와?

은비: 늦게 올 거예요.

- Long Dialogue

엄마: 오늘 집에 언제 들어와? 늦어?

은비: 네. 늦게 올 거예요.

엄마: 어제보다 더 늦게 올 거야?

은비: 아직 몰라요.

엄마: 저녁 먹고 올 거야?

은비: 네. 먹고 올 거예요.

엄마: 일이 많아?

은비: 네. 요즘 일이 많아서 바빠요.

엄마: 그래도 저녁 꼭 먹어야 돼.

은비: 네. 알겠어요.

엄마: 12시 전에 와.

은비: 네. 노력해 볼게요.

Answer Key for grammar exercises

1. 오늘보다 더 *2*. 저녁보다 더 *3*. 하고 오다 *4*. 만나고 오다

Answer Key for pronunciation exercises

1. 낟 *2*. 빋 *3*. 읻꼬 *4*. 빋꽈

Dialogue 08

아침에 깨워 주세요.
Please wake me up in the morning.

Waking Up

Short Dialogue with Translation
Start with a simple, two-line dialogue first!

Track 43

철수: **엄마! 저 내일 여섯 시에 깨워 주세요.**
Mom! Please wake me up at 6 o'clock tomorrow.

엄마: **아침 여섯 시?**
6 o'clock in the morning?

Vocabulary

엄마 [eom-ma]	= mom
저 [jeo]	= I, me
내일 [nae-il]	= tomorrow
여섯 시 [yeo-seot si]	= 6 o'clock
-에 [-e]	= at
깨우다 [kkae-u-da]	= to wake (someone) up
VERB + -아/어/여 주세요. [-a/eo/yeo ju-se-yo.]	= Please VERB (me).
아침 [a-chim]	= morning

Cultural Tip

Since mountains cover almost 70 percent of Korea, many people enjoy hiking as a hobby, especially healthy middle-aged people who have some spare time. Hiking is not as popular with people in their 20-30s, but some bosses like to take their employees on a hike. If you work in Korea and your boss tells you that you are going hiking, Korean work culture makes it difficult to say "no" to your boss, so you just have to join the outing.

Long Dialogue with Translation

Now challenge yourself with a longer dialogue!

◀️)) *Track 45*

철수: 엄마! 저 내일 여섯 시에 깨워 주세요.
Mom! Please wake me up at 6 o'clock tomorrow.

엄마: 아침 여섯 시?
6 o'clock in the morning?

철수: 네. 아침 여섯 시에 일어나야 돼요.
Yes. I need to wake up at 6 o'clock in the morning.

엄마: 왜 그렇게 일찍?
Why so early?

철수: 내일 아침에 등산 갈 거예요.
I will go hiking up the mountain tomorrow morning.

엄마: 내일 너무 추워서 힘들 거야.
It will be difficult because it will be very cold tomorrow.

철수: 괜찮아요. 할 수 있어요.
It's ok. I can do it.

엄마: 누구하고 가?
Who are you going with?

철수: 친구들 세 명이랑 같이 갈 거예요.
I will go with three friends.

엄마: 나도 같이 가자.
Let me go with you.

철수: 안 돼요. 엄마는 힘들 거예요.
No. It will be difficult for you.

엄마: 나도 할 수 있어.
I can do it, too.

Vocabulary

엄마 [eom-ma]	= mom		가다 [ga-da]	= to go
저 [jeo]	= I, me		너무 [neo-mu]	= really, so, too much
내일 [nae-il]	= tomorrow		춥다 [chup-tta]	= to be cold
여섯 시 [yeo-seot si]	= 6 o'clock		힘들다 [him-deul-da]	= to be tough, to be difficult, to be hard
깨워 주다 [kkae-wo ju-da]	= to wake someone up		괜찮다 [gwaen-chan-ta]	= to be ok, to be alright
아침 [a-chim]	= morning		누구 [nu-gu]	= who
일어나다 [i-reo-na-da]	= to wake up		친구들 [chin-gu-deul]	= friends
왜 [wae]	= why		세 명 [se myeong]	= three people
그렇게 [geu-reo-ke]	= so, that		같이 [ga-chi]	= together
일찍 [il-jjik]	= early			
등산 [deung-san]	= hiking, climbing			

Grammar Points & Exercises

Study the two grammar points used in the dialogue and practice!

A. Ability

◀）**Track 47**

VERB + -(으)ㄹ 수 있어요. = I can VERB.

Ex) 하다 + -(으)ㄹ 수 있어요. → 할 수 있어요. = I can do (it).

1. 깨워 주다 + -(으)ㄹ 수 있어요

⋯⋯〉 _____ = I can wake (someone) up.

2. 가다 + -(으)ㄹ 수 있어요

⋯⋯〉 _____ = I can go.

B. Prepositions: "with"

NOUN + -하고 = with NOUN

Ex) 누구 + -하고 → 누구하고 = with whom

3. 친구 + -하고 ⋯⋯〉 _____ = with my friend

4. 아빠 + -하고 ⋯⋯〉 _____ = with my dad

Study the two pronunciation rules used in the dialogue and practice!

A. When ㅅ is used as 받침, or a final consonant, it is pronounced like ㄷ.

◀») *Track 48*

Ex) 여섯 → [여섣]

Write the pronunciations for the following words, just like the above example.

1. 버섯 (mushroom) ······> [   ]

2. 맛 (taste) ······> [   ]

B. When a syllable ends with -(으)ㄹ and is followed by a syllable that begins with ㅅ, ㅅ is pronounced like ㅆ.

Ex) 할 수 → [할 쑤]

Write the pronunciations for the following words, just like the above example.

3. 만날 수 ······> [   ]

4. 볼 수 ······> [   ]

Korean Only

Can you understand the entire dialogue without a translation? Test yourself!

- **Short Dialogue**

철수: 엄마! 저 내일 여섯 시에 깨워 주세요.

엄마: 아침 여섯 시?

- **Long Dialogue**

철수: 엄마! 저 내일 여섯 시에 깨워 주세요.

엄마: 아침 여섯 시?

철수: 네. 아침 여섯 시에 일어나야 돼요.

엄마: 왜 그렇게 일찍?

철수: 내일 아침에 등산 갈 거예요.

엄마: 내일 너무 추워서 힘들 거야.

철수: 괜찮아요. 할 수 있어요.

엄마: 누구하고 가?

철수: 친구들 세 명이랑 같이 갈 거예요.

엄마: 나도 같이 가자.

철수: 안 돼요. 엄마는 힘들 거예요.

엄마: 나도 할 수 있어.

Answer Key for grammar exercises

1. 깨워 줄 수 있어요. *2.* 갈 수 있어요. *3.* 친구하고 *4.* 아빠하고

Answer Key for pronunciation exercises

1. 버섣 *2.* 맏 *3.* 만날 쑤 *4.* 볼 쑤

얼마예요?
How much is it?

•

Marketplace

Short Dialogue with Translation

Start with a simple, two-line dialogue first!

 Track 49

수지: **아저씨, 양파 얼마예요?**
How much are the onions?

상인: **네 개에 삼천 원이에요.**
It's 3,000 won for four.

Vocabulary

아저씨 [a-jeo-ssi]	= *middle-aged man* * You can use **아저씨** when you address a middle-aged man.
양파 [yang-pa]	= *onion*
얼마예요? [eol-ma-ye-yo?]	= *How much is it?*
네 개에 [ne gae-e]	= *for four*
삼천 [sam-cheon]	= *three thousand*
원 [won]	= *unit of Korean money, Korean won(₩)*
NOUN + **-이에요/예요** [-i-e-yo/ye-yo]	= *to be + NOUN*

Cultural Tip

In Korea, fruits and vegetables are typically purchased at one of three places: a street market, small grocery shop, or big supermarket. Since street markets are slowly disappearing, people usually go to a small grocery store nearby or a big supermarket to do their grocery shopping. It is common to see people haggling for the price of produce at most places except big supermarkets.

Long Dialogue with Translation

Now challenge yourself with a longer dialogue!

◀)) *Track 51*

수지: **안녕하세요.**
Hello.

상인: **어서 오세요.**
Welcome.

수지: **아저씨, 양파 어디 있어요?**
Sir, where are the onions?

상인: **양파 여기 있어요.**
The onions are here.

수지: **얼마예요?**
How much are they?

상인: **네 개에 삼천 원이에요.**
It's 3,000 won for four.

수지: **여덟 개 주세요.**
Give me eight, please.

상인: **네. 더 필요한 건 없어요?**
Yes. Is there anything else you need?

수지: **당근은 어디 있어요?**
Where are the carrots?

상인: **당근은 없어요. 다 팔렸어요.**
We don't have carrots. They're sold out.

수지: **아, 그럼 양파만 주세요.**
Oh, then just give me the onions.

상인: **네. 육천 원이에요.**
Ok. It's 6,000 won.

Vocabulary

아저씨
[a-jeo-ssi]
= *middle-aged man*

없다
[eop-tta]
= *to not exist, to not have, to not be there*

양파
[yang-pa]
= *onion*

당근
[dang-geun]
= *carrot*

어디
[eo-di]
= *where*

그럼
[geu-reom]
= *then*

있다
[it-tta]
= *to exist, to have*

육천 원
[yuk-cheon won]
= *six thousand won*

얼마
[eol-ma]
= *how much*

넷
[net]
= *four*

삼천 원
[sam-cheon won]
= *three thousand won*

여덟
[yeo-deol]
= *eight*

주다
[ju-da]
= *to give*

더
[deo]
= *more*

필요하다
[pi-ryo-ha-da]
= *to need*

Grammar Points & Exercises

Study the two grammar points used in the dialogue and practice!

A. Present Tense Interrogative Sentence

◀)) *Track 53*

VERB/ADJECTIVE + -아/어/여요?
= Do/does (SUBJECT) VERB? / Is/am/are (SUBJECT) ADJECTIVE?

Ex) 있다 + -아/어/여요? → 있어요? = Do you have …? / Are there …?

1. 없다 + -아/어/여요? ……⟩ _____ = Do you not have (it)?

2. 필요하다 + -아/어/여요? ……⟩ _____ = Do you need (it)?

B. Modifier: "only"

NOUN + -만 = NOUN only

Ex) 양파 + -만 → 양파만 = onions only

3. 당근 + -만 ……⟩ _____ = carrots only

4. 아저씨 + -만 ……⟩ _____ = middle-aged men only

Study the two pronunciation rules used in the dialogue and practice!

A. When a word or syllable ends with ㄼ and is followed by a consonant, only ㄹ is pronounced, not ㅂ.

Ex) 여덟 → [여덜]

B. When ㄼ is pronounced as ㄹ and is followed by a syllable that begins with ㄱ, the ㄱ is pronounced as ㄲ.

Ex) 여덟 개 → [여덜 깨]

Write the pronunciations for the following words, just like the above example.

1. 넓게 (widely) ┈┈> [   ]

2. 넓고 (wide and...) ┈┈> [   ]

Korean Only
Can you understand the entire dialogue without a translation? Test yourself!

- Short Dialogue

수지: 아저씨, 양파 얼마예요?

아저씨: 네 개에 삼천 원이에요.

- Long Dialogue

수지: 안녕하세요.

상인: 어서 오세요.

수지: 아저씨, 양파 어디 있어요?

상인: 양파 여기 있어요.

수지: 얼마예요?

상인: 네 개에 삼천 원이에요.

수지: 여덟 개 주세요.

상인: 네. 더 필요한 건 없어요?

수지: 당근은 어디 있어요?

상인: 당근은 없어요. 다 팔렸어요.

수지: 아, 그럼 양파만 주세요.

상인: 네. 육천 원이에요.

Answer Key for grammar exercises
1. 없어요? *2.* 필요해요? *3.* 당근만 *4.* 아저씨만

Answer Key for pronunciation exercises
1. 널께 *2.* 널꼬

더 큰 거 있어요?

Do you have something bigger?

·

Clothing Store

Short Dialogue with Translation

Start with a simple, two-line dialogue first!

 Track 55

상미: **이거 입어 볼 수 있어요?**
Can I try this on?

점원: **네. 입어 보세요.**
Yes, please try it on.

Vocabulary

이거 [i-geo]	= this, this thing
입다 [ip-tta]	= to wear, to put on
VERB + -아/어/여 보다 [-a/eo/yeo bo-da]	= to try out VERB-ing
-(으)ㄹ 수 있다 [-(eu)l su it-tta]	= can, to be able to
네. [ne.]	= Yes.
-(으)세요 [-(eu)-se-yo]	= imperative ending (polite)

Cultural Tip

At some small independent clothing stores in Korea, often times you are not allowed to try on clothes before you make a purchase, especially with t-shirts. This is usually because the neck part could get stretched, or your makeup or sweat could wipe off on the t-shirt.

Long Dialogue with Translation

Now challenge yourself with a longer dialogue!

점원: **어서 오세요.**
Welcome.

Track 57

상미: **네. 안녕하세요.**
Yes. Hi.

점원: **뭐 찾으세요?**
What are you looking for?

상미: **치마요.**
A skirt.

점원: **치마는 여기에 있어요. 여기 보세요.**
Skirts are here. Look here.

상미: **네. 이거 다른 색깔은 없나요?**
Ok. Do you have any other colors?

점원: **이건 검은색이랑 빨간색밖에 없어요.**
This one only comes in black and red.

상미: **이거 입어 볼 수 있어요?**
Can I try it on?

점원: **네. 입어 보세요.**
Yes, please try it on.

상미: **사이즈가 작아요. 더 큰 거 있어요?**
It's too small. Do you have something bigger?

점원: **네, 어떤 사이즈요?**
Yes. What size?

상미: **허리 27사이즈요.**
Waist size 27.

Vocabulary

뭐
[mwo]
= what

찾다
[chat-tta]
= to find, to look for

치마
[chi-ma]
= skirt

여기
[yeo-gi]
= here

있다
[it-tta]
= to exist, to have

보다
[bo-da]
= to see, to watch

이거
[i-geo]
= this, this thing

다른
[da-reun]
= different

색깔
[saek-kkal]
= color

없다
[eop-tta]
= to not exist, to not have, to not be there

검은색
[geo-meun-saek]
= black color

빨간색
[ppal-gan-saek]
= red color

입어 보다
[i-beo bo-da]
= to try on

사이즈
[ssa-i-jeu]
= size

작다
[jak-tta]
= to be small

더
[deo]
= more

크다
[keu-da]
= to be big

어떤
[eo-tteon]
= which

허리
[heo-ri]
= waist

Grammar Points & Exercises

Study the two grammar points used in the dialogue and practice!

A. Conjunction: "and"

NOUN + -(이)랑 : NOUN and NOUN

Ex) 검은색 + -(이)랑 + 빨간색 → 검은색이랑 빨간색 = black and red

1. 치마 + -(이)랑 + 바지 ······> _____ = a skirt and pants

2. 가족 + -(이)랑 + 친구 ······> _____ = family and a friend

B. Modifier: "nothing but" or "only"

NOUN + -밖에 : nothing but NOUN / only NOUN

* This is always followed by a negative expression.

Ex) 빨간색 + -밖에 → 빨간색밖에 = nothing but red color / only red color

3. 이거 + -밖에 ······> _____ = nothing but this one / only this one

4. 친구 + -밖에 ······> _____ = nothing but a friend / only a friend

Study the two pronunciation rules used in the dialogue and practice!

A. When a word or syllable ends with ㅄ and is followed by a consonant, only ㅂ is pronounced, not ㅅ.

◀) *Track 60*

Ex) 없 → [업]

B. When ㅄ is followed by a syllable that begins with a vowel, the ㅅ becomes part of the following syllable and is pronounced as ㅆ.

Ex) 없어요 → [업써요]

Write the pronunciations for the following words, just like the above example.

1. 값 (price) ······> [   ]

2. 값이 (the price is ···) ······> [   ]

Can you understand the entire dialogue without a translation? Test yourself!

- Short Dialogue

상미: 이거 입어 볼 수 있어요?

점원: 네. 입어 보세요.

- Long Dialogue

점원: 어서 오세요.

상미: 네. 안녕하세요.

점원: 뭐 찾으세요?

상미: 치마요.

점원: 치마는 여기에 있어요. 여기 보세요.

상미: 네. 이거 다른 색깔은 없나요?

점원: 이건 검은색이랑 빨간색밖에 없어요.

상미: 이거 입어 볼 수 있어요?

점원: 네. 입어 보세요.

상미: 사이즈가 작아요. 더 큰 거 있어요?

점원: 네, 어떤 사이즈요?

상미: 허리 27사이즈요.

Answer Key for grammar exercises

1. 치마랑 바지 *2.* 가족이랑 친구 *3.* 이거밖에 *4.* 친구밖에

Answer Key for pronunciation exercises

1. 갑 *2.* 갑씨

이거 살게요.

I will buy this.

•

Shoe Store

Short Dialogue with Translation

Start with a simple, two-line dialogue first!

 Track 61

미선: 이 구두 다른 색깔은 없어요?
Are there no other colors for these shoes?

점원: 네. 이 색깔밖에 없어요.
Yes. Only this color.

Vocabulary

이 [i]	= *this, these*
구두 [gu-du]	= *dress shoes*
다른 [da-reun]	= *different*
색깔 [saek-kkal]	= *color*
없다 [eop-tta]	= *to not exist, to not have, to not be there*
네. [ne]	= *Yes. / No.* * "네" has the same meaning as "no" when confirming a negative question.
-밖에 [-ba-kke]	= *nothing but, only*

Cultural Tip

If you need speedy shoe repair in Korea, it is best to visit one of the tiny shoe repair shops on the street rather than leaving/sending your shoes off to the brand's repair service. Some brands offer free repair service for their shoes, but it typically takes 1-2 weeks to get them back.

Long Dialogue with Translation

Now challenge yourself with a longer dialogue!

미선: **와! 이 구두 예쁘다. 그런데 이 구두 다른 색깔은 없어요?**   🔊) *Track 63*
Wow! These shoes are pretty. But are there no other colors for these shoes?

점원: **네. 이 색깔밖에 없어요.**
Yes. Only this color.

미선: **이거 신어 봐도 돼요?**
May I try them on?

점원: **네. 신어 보세요. 사이즈가 어떻게 되세요?**
Yes, please try them on. What is your size?

미선: **230mm요.**
230mm.

점원: **아, 230mm는 없어요.**
Oh, we don't have 230mm.

미선: **그럼 235mm는 있어요?**
Then do you have 235mm?

점원: **네. 있어요. 잠시만요.**
Yes, we do. Wait a moment.

(a few minutes later)

점원: **여기요. 신어 보세요.**
Here. Please try them on.

미선: **조금 커요. 그래도 마음에 들어요.**
They are a bit big. But I still like them.

점원: **정말 예뻐요.**
They are so pretty.

미선: **이거 살게요. 얼마예요?**
I'll buy them. How much are they?

Vocabulary

이
[i]
= this, these

구두
[gu-du]
= dress shoes

예쁘다
[ye-ppeu-da]
= to be pretty

그런데
[geu-reon-de]
= but, however

다른
[da-reun]
= different

색깔
[saek-kkal]
= color

없다
[eop-tta]
= to not exist, to not
  have, to not be there

신어 보다
[si-neo bo-da]
= to try on shoes

잠시
[jam-si]
= for a moment, briefly

조금
[jo-geum]
= a little

크다
[keu-da]
= to be big

그래도
[geu-rae-do]
= even so, nevertheless

마음에 들다
[ma-eu-me deul-da]
= to like

정말
[jeong-mal]
= really, very

사다
[sa-da]
= to buy

얼마
[eol-ma]
= how much

Grammar Points & Exercises

Study the two grammar points used in the dialogue and practice!

A. Asking Permission

VERB + -아/어/여도 돼요? = May I VERB?

Ex) 신어 보다 + -아/어/여도 돼요? → 신어 봐도 돼요? = May I try the shoes on?

1. 사다 + -아/어/여도 돼요? ······⟩ _____ = May I buy (it)?

2. 먹다 + -아/어/여도 돼요? ······⟩ _____ = May I eat (it)?

B. Imperative Sentence Ending - Honorific

VERB + -(으)세요. = Please VERB. / VERB, please.

Ex) 신어 보다 + -(으)세요 → 신어 보세요. = Please try on the shoes.

3. 공부하다 + -(으)세요 ······⟩ _____ = Study, please.

4. 기다리다 + -(으)세요······⟩ _____ = Wait, please.

Study the two pronunciation rules used in the dialogue and practice!

A. According to Korean loanword orthography, loanwords are written using the 24 basic letters, not the five tense consonants: ㄲ, ㄸ, ㅃ, ㅆ, and ㅉ. This leads to many loanwords being written differently than how they are pronounced.

Ex) 사이즈 (size) → [싸이즈]

게임 (game) → [께임]

B. When a syllable ends with ㅁ and is followed by a syllable that begins with a vowel, the ㅁ becomes part of the following syllable rather than being pronounced distinctly as two different syllables.

Ex) 마음에 → [마으메]

Write the pronunciations for the following words, just like the above example.

1. 조금은 ······> [   ]

2. 검은색 ······> [   ]

Korean Only
Can you understand the entire dialogue without a translation? Test yourself!

- *Short Dialogue*

미선: 이 구두 다른 색깔은 없어요?

점원: 네. 이 색깔밖에 없어요.

- *Long Dialogue*

미선: 와! 이 구두 예쁘다. 그런데 이 구두 다른 색깔은 없어요?

점원: 네. 이 색깔밖에 없어요.

미선: 이거 신어 봐도 돼요?

정배: 네. 신어 보세요. 사이즈가 어떻게 되세요?

미선: 230mm요.

점원: 아, 230mm는 없어요.

미선: 그럼 235mm는 있어요?

점원: 네. 있어요. 잠시만요.

점원: 여기요. 신어 보세요.

미선: 조금 커요. 그래도 마음에 들어요.

점원: 정말 예뻐요.

미선: 이거 살게요. 얼마예요?

Answer Key for grammar exercises

1. 사도 돼요? *2*. 먹어도 돼요? *3*. 공부하세요. *4*. 기다리세요.

Answer Key for pronunciation exercises

1. 조그믄 *2*. 거믄색

카메라 사고 싶어요.
I want to buy a camera.

Electronics Store

Short Dialogue with Translation

Start with a simple, two-line dialogue first!

 Track 67

점원: **어떤 거 찾으세요?**
What type of thing are you looking for?

소율: **카메라 찾고 있어요.**
I am looking for a camera.

Vocabulary

어떤 거 [eo-tteon geo]	= *which one, what type of thing, what kind of stuff*
찾다 [chat-tta]	= *to find, to look for*
카메라 [ka-me-ra]	= *camera*
VERB + **-고 있다** [-go it-tta]	= *to be VERB-ing*

Cultural Tip

There is a growing trend in Korea to buy electronics online, since there is usually a seller who offers an item for a cheaper price than in a store. Buying electronics via TV home shopping is also quite common since many electronics companies make cheaper products exclusively for home shopping channels.

Long Dialogue with Translation

Now challenge yourself with a longer dialogue!

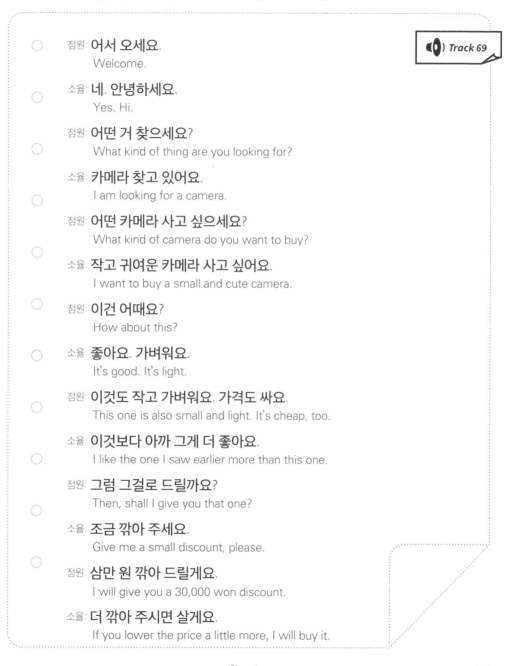

점원: 어서 오세요.
Welcome.

Track 69

소율: 네. 안녕하세요.
Yes. Hi.

점원: 어떤 거 찾으세요?
What kind of thing are you looking for?

소율: 카메라 찾고 있어요.
I am looking for a camera.

점원: 어떤 카메라 사고 싶으세요?
What kind of camera do you want to buy?

소율: 작고 귀여운 카메라 사고 싶어요.
I want to buy a small and cute camera.

점원: 이건 어때요?
How about this?

소율: 좋아요. 가벼워요.
It's good. It's light.

점원: 이것도 작고 가벼워요. 가격도 싸요.
This one is also small and light. It's cheap, too.

소율: 이것보다 아까 그게 더 좋아요.
I like the one I saw earlier more than this one.

점원: 그럼 그걸로 드릴까요?
Then, shall I give you that one?

소율: 조금 깎아 주세요.
Give me a small discount, please.

점원: 삼만 원 깎아 드릴게요.
I will give you a 30,000 won discount.

소율: 더 깎아 주시면 살게요.
If you lower the price a little more, I will buy it.

Vocabulary

어떤 거 [eo-tteon geo]	= *which one, what type of thing, what kind of stuff*
찾다 [chat-tta]	= *to find, to look for*
카메라 [ka-me-ra]	= *camera*
사다 [sa-da]	= *to buy*
작다 [jak-tta]	= *to be small*
귀엽다 [gwi-yeop-tta]	= *to be cute*
좋다 [jo-ta]	= *to be good, to like*
가볍다 [ga-byeop-tta]	= *to be light*
가격 [ga-gyeok]	= *price*
싸다 [ssa-da]	= *to be cheap*
아까 [a-kka]	= *earlier*

그것 [geu-geot]	= *that one*
더 [deo]	= *more*
그럼 [geu-reom]	= *then*
드리다 [deu-ri-da]	= *to give (honorific)*
깎아 주다 [kka-kka ju-da]	= *to give a discount*

Grammar Points & Exercises

Study the two grammar points used in the dialogue and practice!

A. To Want

VERB + -고 싶어요. = I want to VERB.

> **Ex)** 사다 + -고 싶어요 → 사고 싶어요. = I want to buy (it).

> **1.** 드리다 + -고 싶어요 ……⟩ _____ = I want to give (it).

> **2.** 깎아 주다 + -고 싶어요 ……⟩ _____ = I want to give a discount.

B. Conjunction: "and"

VERB/ADJECTIVE + -고 + VERB/ADJECTIVE
= VERB/ADJECTIVE and VERB/ADJECTIVE

> **Ex)** 작다 + -고 + 가볍다 → 작고 가볍다 = to be small and light

> **3.** 귀엽다 + -고 + 싸다 ……⟩ _____ = to be cute and cheap

> **4.** 크다 + -고 + 좋다……⟩ _____ = to be big and good

Study the two pronunciation rules used in the dialogue and practice!

A. When a syllable ends with ㄲ and is followed by a syllable that begins with a vowel, ㄲ becomes part of the following syllable rather than being pronounced distinctly as two different syllables.

Ex) 깎아 → [까까]

Write the pronunciations for the following words, just like the above example.

1. 볶아 ······> [   ]

2. 밖에 ······> [   ]

B. When a syllable has ㅅ as the 받침, it is pronounced like ㄷ. If the following syllable begins with ㄷ, it is pronounced as ㄸ.

Ex) 이것도 → [이걷또]

* If you are wondering why ㅅ is pronounced like ㄷ, please refer to page 74.

Write the pronunciations for the following words, just like the above example.

3. 웃다 (to smile, to laugh) ······> [   ]

4. 붓다 (to pour) ······> [   ]

Korean Only

Can you understand the entire dialogue without a translation? Test yourself!

- Short Dialogue

점원: 어떤 거 찾으세요?

소율: 카메라 찾고 있어요.

- Long Dialogue

점원: 어서 오세요.

소율: 네. 안녕하세요.

점원: 어떤 거 찾으세요?

소율: 카메라 찾고 있어요.

점원: 어떤 카메라 사고 싶으세요?

소율: 작고 귀여운 카메라 사고 싶어요.

점원: 이건 어때요?

소율: 좋아요. 가벼워요.

점원: 이것도 작고 가벼워요. 가격도 싸요.

소율: 이것보다 아까 그게 더 좋아요.

점원: 그럼 그걸로 드릴까요?

소율: 조금 깎아 주세요.

점원: 삼만 원 깎아 드릴게요.

소율: 더 깎아 주시면 살게요.

Answer Key for grammar exercises

1. 드리고 싶어요. *2.* 깎아 주고 싶어요. *3.* 귀엽고 싸다 *4.* 크고 좋다

Answer Key for pronunciation exercises

1. 보까 *2.* 바께 *3.* 운따 *4.* 붇따

이 침대 얼마예요?
How much is this bed?

•

Furniture Store

Short Dialogue with Translation
Start with a simple, two-line dialogue first!

 Track 73

손님: 이 침대 얼마예요?
How much is this bed?

점원: 이건 오백만 원이에요.
It's 5 million won.

Vocabulary

이 [i]	= *this, these*
침대 [chim-dae]	= *bed*
얼마 [eol-ma]	= *how much*
이건 [i-geon]	= *this, this thing* * 이건 is short for 이것은, which is 이것 followed by the topic marker 은.
오백만 [o-baeng-man]	= *5 million*
원 [won]	= *unit of Korean money, Korean won (₩)*

Cultural Tip

Sleeping on a bed only became a common practice in Korea during the 1990s. Older generations of Koreans still find it comfortable to sleep on the heated floor, known as 온돌 (on-dol). For that reason, many middle-aged Korean people often buy a stone or soil bed with a hard surface (no mattress) that can be heated, just like a traditional Korean floor.

Long Dialogue with Translation

Now challenge yourself with a longer dialogue!

손님: 이 침대 얼마예요?
How much is this bed?

Track 75

점원: 이건 오백만 원이에요.
It's 5 million won.

손님: 비싸네요. 더 싼 거 있어요?
It's expensive. Do you have something cheaper?

점원: 네. 있어요. 그럼 이건 어떠세요?
Yes, we do. Then, how about this one?

손님: 이건 그것보다 사이즈가 좀 작네요. 가격이 더 싸요?
This one is a little smaller than that one. Is it cheaper?

점원: 네. 아주 싸요. 사백구십만 원이에요.
Yes, it's very cheap. It's 4 million, 9 hundred thousand won.

손님: 별로 안 싸네요. 세일 안 해요?
It's not that cheap. Is there no sale?

점원: 지금은 세일 안 해요.
We are not having a sale yet.

손님: 언제 세일해요?
When are you having a sale?

점원: 아직은 계획이 없어요. 세일하면 연락드릴게요.
We don't have any plans yet. I will let you know when we do.

손님: 네. 침대 배달해 주세요?
Yes. Do you deliver your beds?

점원: 네. 배달해 드려요.
Yes, we deliver them.

Vocabulary

침대 [chim-dae]	= bed	아주 [a-ju]	= very
얼마 [eol-ma]	= how much	사백구십만 [sa-baek-gu-sim-man]	= 4 million, 9 hundred thousand
오백만 [o-baeng-man]	= 5 million	별로 [byeol-lo]	= not so much
비싸다 [bi-ssa-da]	= to be expensive	세일 [sse-il]	= sale
더 [deo]	= more	하다 [ha-da]	= to do
싸다 [ssa-da]	= to be cheap	지금 [ji-geum]	= now
있다 [it-tta]	= to exist, to have	언제 [eon-je]	= when
그럼 [geu-reom]	= then	아직 [a-jik]	= yet
이것 [i-geot]	= this, this thing	계획 [gye-hoek]	= plan
좀 [jom]	= a little bit	없다 [eop-tta]	= to not exist, to not have, to not be there
작다 [jak-tta]	= to be small	연락드리다 [yeol-lak-deu-ri-da]	= to contact, to let (someone) know (honorific)
가격 [ga-gyeok]	= price	배달하다 [bae-da-ra-da]	= to deliver

Grammar Points & Exercises

Study the two grammar points used in the dialogue and practice!

A. Expressing Your Impression

VERB/ADJECTIVE + -네요.
= (Oh, I see that) it is VERB/ADJECTIVE.

Ex) 작다 + -네요 → 작네요 = (Oh, I see that) it is small.

1. 안 싸다 + -네요 ······⟩ _____ = (Oh, I see that) it is not cheap.

2. 세일하다 + -네요 ······⟩ _____ = (Oh, I see that) it is on sale.

B. Conjunction: "if"

VERB + -(으)면 = if (SUBJECT) VERB

Ex) 세일하다 + -(으)면 → 세일하면 = if we have a sale

3. 없다 + -(으)면 ······⟩ _____ = if there is not

4. 배달하다 + -(으)면······⟩ _____ = if you deliver

Study the two pronunciation rules used in the dialogue and practice!

A. When a syllable ends with ㄱ and is followed by a syllable that begins with ㅁ, the ㄱ is pronounced as ㅇ.

Ex) 백만원 → [뱅마뉜]

* If you are wondering why 만원 is pronounced as 마뉜, please refer to page 50.

Write the pronunciations for the following words, just like the above example.

1. 국물 (soup) ······> [   ]

2. 곡물 (grain, cereal) ······> [   ]

B. When a syllable ends with ㅂ and is followed by a syllable that begins with ㅁ, the ㅂ is pronounced as ㅁ.

Ex) 사백구십만 → [사백구심만]

Write the pronunciations for the following words, just like the above example.

3. 집문서 (house deed) ······> [   ]

4. 입맛 (appetite) ······> [   ]

Korean Only

Can you understand the entire dialogue without a translation? Test yourself!

- Short Dialogue

손님: 이 침대 얼마예요?

점원: 이건 오백만 원이에요.

- Long Dialogue

손님: 이 침대 얼마예요?

점원: 이건 오백만 원이에요.

손님: 비싸네요. 더 싼 거 있어요?

점원: 네. 있어요. 그럼 이건 어떠세요?

손님: 이건 그것보다 사이즈가 좀 작네요. 가격이 더 싸요?

점원: 네. 아주 싸요. 사백구십만 원이에요.

손님: 별로 안 싸네요. 세일 안 해요?

점원: 지금은 세일 안 해요.

손님: 언제 세일해요?

점원: 아직은 계획이 없어요. 세일하면 연락드릴게요.

손님: 네. 침대 배달해 주세요?

점원: 네. 배달해 드려요.

Answer Key for grammar exercises

1. 안 싸네요. *2.* 세일하네요. *3.* 없으면 *4.* 배달하면

Answer Key for pronunciation exercises

1. 궁물 *2.* 공물 *3.* 짐문서 *4.* 임맏*

* *If you are wondering why* 맛 *is pronounced as* 맏, *please refer to page 74.*

영수증 여기 있습니다.
Here is your receipt.

Cosmetics Store

Track 79

Short Dialogue with Translation

Start with a simple, two-line dialogue first!

손님: **토너하고 로션 추천해 주세요.**
Please recommend a toner and a lotion.

점원: **네. 피부가 지성이에요? 건성이에요?**
Ok. Do you have oily or dry skin?

Vocabulary

토너 [to-neo]	= toner		**네.** [ne.]	= Ok. / Yes.
-하고 [-ha-go]	= and		**피부** [pi-bu]	= skin
로션 [lo-syeon]	= lotion		**지성** [ji-seong]	= oily skin
추천하다 [chu-cheo-na-da]	= to recommend		**건성** [geon-seong]	= dry skin
VERB + **-아/어/여 주세요.** [-a/eo/yeo ju-se-yo.]	= Please VERB (me).			
A-**이/가** B-**이에요/예요?** [A-i/ga B-i-e-yo/ye-yo?]	= Is A B?			

Cultural Tip

You will see a multitude of cosmetic stores while walking down the street in Korea. Most stores have good quality and affordable products. In addition to cosmetic stores, there are also drugstores. Drugstores carry affordable cosmetics and skincare products from Korea as well as other countries, such as Japan, France, or Germany. If you are looking to purchase more luxury or high-end brands of cosmetics or skincare products, visit a department store.

Long Dialogue with Translation

Now challenge yourself with a longer dialogue!

🔊 *Track 81*

손님: 토너하고 로션 추천해 주세요.
Please recommend a toner and a lotion.

점원: 네. 피부가 지성이세요? 건성이세요?
Ok. Do you have oily or dry skin?

손님: 건성이에요.
I have dry skin.

점원: 그럼 이거 써 보세요. 촉촉한 로션이에요.
Then try using this. It's a moisturizer.

손님: 고맙습니다. 이거 세 개 주세요.
Thank you. Please give me three of these.

점원: 두 개밖에 없어요. 다 떨어졌어요.
We only have two. We ran out of the rest.

손님: 아, 그래요? 그럼 두 개만 주세요.
Oh, really? Then, just give me two.

점원: 네. 삼만 원입니다.
Ok. It's 30,000 won.

손님: 여기요.
Here.

점원: 삼만 원 받았습니다. 포인트 적립해 드릴까요?
I've received 30,000 won. Shall I add points to your points account?

손님: 아니요, 괜찮아요.
No, it's ok.

점원: 네, 영수증 여기 있습니다. 감사합니다.
Ok. Here is your receipt. Thank you.

손님: 네, 수고하세요.
Ok. Bye.

Vocabulary

토너
[to-neo]
= toner

로션
[lo-syeon]
= lotion

추천하다
[chu-cheo-na-da]
= to recommend

피부
[pi-bu]
= skin

지성
[ji-seong]
= oily skin

건성
[geon-seong]
= dry skin

그럼
[geu-reom]
= then

이거
[i-geo]
= this, this thing

쓰다
[sseu-da]
= to use

써 보다
[sseo bo-da]
= to try using

촉촉하다
[chok-cho-ka-da]
= to be moist

고맙다
[go-map-tta]
= to be thankful

세 개
[se gae]
= three things

주다
[ju-da]
= to give

다
[da]
= all

떨어지다
[tteo-reo-ji-da]
= to run out of something

삼만
[sam-man]
= 30 thousand

여기
[yeo-gi]
= here

받다
[bat-tta]
= to receive

포인트
[po-in-teu]
= mileage, point

적립하다
[jeong-ni-pa-da]
= to accumulate

괜찮다
[gwaen-chan-ta]
= to be ok, to be alright

영수증
[yeong-su-jeung]
= receipt

Grammar Points & Exercises

Study the two grammar points used in the dialogue and practice!

A. To Experiment / Try With an Action

VERB + -아/어/여 보세요. = Try VERB-ing.

Ex) 쓰다 + -아/어/여 보세요 → 써 보세요. = Try using (it).

1. 추천하다 + -아/어/여 보세요 ……> _____ = Try recommending (it).

2. 받다 + -아/어/여 보세요 ……> _____ = Try receiving (it).

B. Suggestion

VERB + -아/어/여 드릴까요? = Shall I VERB (for you)?

Ex) 적립하다 + -아/어/여 드릴까요?

→ 적립해 드릴까요? = Shall I add (points for you)?

3. 추천하다 + -아/어/여 드릴까요?

……> _____ = Shall I recommend you (it)?

4. 사다 + -아/어/여 드릴까요?

……> _____ = Shall I buy you (it)?

Study the two pronunciation rules used in the dialogue and practice!

A. When a syllable ends with ㄱ and is followed by a syllable that begins with ㄹ, the ㄹ is pronounced as ㄴ.

Ex) 적립 → [적닙]

B. When a syllable ends with ㄱ and is followed by a syllable that begins with ㄴ, the ㄱ is pronounced as ㅇ.

Ex) [적닙] → [정닙]

Write the pronunciations for the following words, just like the above example.

1. 독립 (independence) ······> [   ]

2. 복리 (welfare, well-being) ······> [   ]

Korean Only

Can you understand the entire dialogue without a translation? Test yourself!

- Short Dialogue

손님: 토너하고 로션 추천해 주세요.

점원: 네. 피부가 지성이에요? 건성이에요?

- Long Dialogue

손님: 토너하고 로션 추천해 주세요.

점원: 네. 피부가 지성이세요? 건성이세요?

손님: 건성이에요.

점원: 그럼 이거 써 보세요. 촉촉한 로션이에요.

손님: 고맙습니다. 이거 세 개 주세요.

점원: 두 개밖에 없어요. 다 떨어졌어요.

손님: 아, 그래요? 그럼 두 개만 주세요.

점원: 네. 삼만 원입니다.

손님: 여기요.

점원: 삼만 원 받았습니다. 포인트 적립해 드릴까요?

손님: 아니요, 괜찮아요.

점원: 네, 영수증 여기 있습니다. 감사합니다.

손님: 네, 수고하세요.

Answer Key for grammar exercises

1. 추천해 보세요. *2.* 받아 보세요. *3.* 추천해 드릴까요? *4.* 사 드릴까요?

Answer Key for pronunciation exercises

1. 동닙 *2.* 봉니

Dialogue 15

이 책은 지금 없어요.

We don't have this book now.

•

Bookstore

Short Dialogue with Translation
Start with a simple, two-line dialogue first!

손님: 이 책 언제 살 수 있어요?
When can I buy this book?

점원: 다음 주에 다시 오세요.
Come again next week.

Vocabulary

이 [i]	= this, these	주 [ju]	= week
책 [chaek]	= book	-에 [-e]	= at, in
언제 [eon-je]	= when	다시 [da-si]	= again
사다 [sa-da]	= to buy	오다 [o-da]	= to come
다음 [da-eum]	= next	-(으)세요 [-(eu)-se-yo]	= imperative ending (polite)
VERB + -(으)ㄹ 수 있어요? [-(eu)l su i-sseo-yo?]	= Can I/you VERB?		

Cultural Tip

Online bookstores in Korea, which usually offered big discounts on new books, were growing in popularity until the government introduced a new "book price control system" in 2014. The new system restricts the discount rate of new books to a maximum of 10 percent of the cover price. As a result, more people started to buy secondhand books. To meet the increase in demand, online booksellers have begun opening up secondhand bookstores in busy areas in Korea.

Long Dialogue with Translation
Now challenge yourself with a longer dialogue!

Track 87

손님: 저기요. 이 책을 찾고 있는데 못 찾겠어요.
Excuse me. I'm looking for this book, but I can't find it.

점원: 이 책은 지금 없어요. 이 책이 인기가 많아서 다 팔렸어요.
We don't have this book now. This book is popular, so it's sold out.

손님: 그럼 언제 살 수 있어요?
Then, when can I buy it?

점원: 아직 모르겠어요. 다른 서점에 있을 수도 있어요.
I don't know yet. Other bookstores might have it.

손님: 다른 서점은 못 가요. 여기에서 사야 돼요.
I can't go to other bookstores. I have to buy it here.

점원: 그럼 기다려야 돼요.
Then you need to wait.

손님: 언제까지 기다려야 해요?
Until when do I have to wait?

점원: 다음 주에 다시 오세요.
Come again next week.

손님: 다음 주에는 책을 살 수 있어요?
Can I buy the book next week?

점원: 그럴 것 같아요.
I think so.

손님: 확실하지 않아요?
You are not sure?

점원: 네. 확실하지 않아요.
Right. I'm not sure.

Vocabulary

저기요
[jeo-gi-yo]
= Excuse me

모르다
[mo-reu-da]
= to not know

책
[chaek]
= book

다른
[da-reun]
= different

찾다
[chat-tta]
= to find, to look for

서점
[seo-jeom]
= bookstore

지금
[ji-geum]
= now

있다
[it-tta]
= to exist, to have

없다
[eop-tta]
= to not exist, to not have, to not be there

여기
[yeo-gi]
= here

인기가 많다
[in-kki-ga man-ta]
= to be popular

다음
[da-eum]
= next

다 팔리다
[da pal-li-da]
= to be sold out

주
[ju]
= week

그럼
[geu-reom]
= then

다시
[da-si]
= again

언제
[eon-je]
= when

오다
[o-da]
= to come

사다
[sa-da]
= to buy

확실하다
[hwak-ssi-ra-da]
= to be sure

아직
[a-jik]
= yet

Grammar Points & Exercises

Study the two grammar points used in the dialogue and practice!

A. Cannot Do Something

못 + VERB + -아/어/여요. = I can't VERB.

Ex) 못 + 가다 + -아/어/여요 → 못 가요. = I can't go.

1. 못 + 사다 + -아/어/여요 ⋯⋯〉

_____ = I can't buy (it).

2. 못 + 오다 + -아/어/여요 ⋯⋯〉

_____ = I can't come.

B. Conjunction: "but"

VERB/ADJECTIVE + -(으)ㄴ/는데 ⋯ = ... but ...

Ex) 찾고 있다 + -(으)ㄴ/는데 + 못 찾겠어요

→ 찾고 있는데 못 찾겠어요. = I'm looking for (it), but I can't find it.

3. 인기가 없다 + -(으)ㄴ/는데 + 다 팔렸어요

⋯⋯〉 _____ = It's not popular, but it's sold out.

4. 배고프다 + -(으)ㄴ/는데 + 음식이 없어요

⋯⋯〉 _____ = I'm hungry, but there's no food.

Study the two pronunciation rules used in the dialogue and practice!

A. When a syllable ends with ㅆ (which sounds the same as ㄷ when in the 받침 position) and is followed by a syllable that begins with ㄴ, the ㅆ is pronounced as ㄴ.

◀) *Track 90*

Ex) 있는데 → [읻는데] → [인는데]

Write the pronunciations for the following words, just like the above example.

1. 갔는데 ……> [   ]

2. 봤는데 ……> [   ]

B. When a syllable ends with ㅅ (which sounds the same as ㄷ when in the 받침 position) and is followed by a syllable that begins with ㄱ, the ㄱ is pronounced as ㄲ.

Ex) 못 가요 → [몯 까요]

* If you are wondering why 못 is pronounced as 몯, please refer to page 74.

Write the pronunciations for the following words, just like the above example.

1. 웃고 ……> [   ]

2. 짓기 ……> [   ]

Korean Only

Can you understand the entire dialogue without a translation? Test yourself!

- Short Dialogue

손님: 이 책 언제 살 수 있어요?

점원: 다음 주에 다시 오세요.

- Long Dialogue

손님: 저기요. 이 책을 찾고 있는데 못 찾겠어요.

점원: 이 책은 지금 없어요. 이 책이 인기가 많아서 다 팔렸어요.

손님: 그럼 언제 살 수 있어요?

점원: 아직 모르겠어요. 다른 서점에 있을 수도 있어요.

손님: 다른 서점은 못 가요. 여기에서 사야 돼요.

점원: 그럼 기다려야 돼요.

손님: 언제까지 기다려야 해요?

점원: 다음 주에 다시 오세요.

손님: 다음 주에는 책을 살 수 있어요?

점원: 그럴 것 같아요.

손님: 확실하지 않아요?

점원: 네. 확실하지 않아요.

Answer Key for grammar exercises

1. 못 사요. *2.* 못 와요. *3.* 인기가 없는데 다 팔렸어요. *4.* 배고픈데 음식이 없어요.

Answer Key for pronunciation exercises

1. 간는데 *2.* 봔는데 *3.* 웉꼬 *4.* 짙끼

Dialogue 16

취미가 뭐예요?
What is your hobby?

•

Blind Date

Short Dialogue with Translation

Start with a simple, two-line dialogue first!

인성: **선주 씨는 취미가 뭐예요?**
Seonju, what is your hobby?

선주: **저는 책 읽는 거 좋아해요.**
I like reading books.

On a Date

Vocabulary

씨 [ssi]	= *honorific suffix which implies respect toward the person whose name it is attached to*
취미 [chwi-mi]	= *hobby*
NOUN + -이/가 뭐예요? [-i/ga mwo-ye-yo?]	= *What is NOUN?*
저 [jeo]	= *I, me*
책 [chaek]	= *book*
읽다 [ik-tta]	= *to read*
VERB + -는 거 [-neun geo]	= *VERB-ing, the act of VERB-ing*
좋아하다 [jo-a-ha-da]	= *to like*

Cultural Tip

Blind dates are fairly common in Korea due to the societal norm to keep to oneself and not strike up a conversation with a stranger. People in their early 20s may go on a blind date to find a boy/girlfriend, but people who have already graduated from university tend to be a bit more serious about blind dates, so serious that they allow their close friends and relatives to set them up with someone as a marriage prospect.

Long Dialogue with Translation
Now challenge yourself with a longer dialogue!

Track 93

인성: 선주 씨는 취미가 뭐예요?
Seonju, what is your hobby?

선주: 저는 책 읽는 거 좋아해요. 인성 씨는 뭐 좋아하세요?
I like reading books. In-seong, what do you like?

인성: 저는 운동 좋아해요.
I like to work out.

선주: 아, 어떤 운동을 잘하세요?
Oh, what exercise do you do well?

인성: 저는 농구를 제일 잘해요. 선주 씨도 운동 좋아하세요?
I play basketball well. Seonju, do you also like to work out?

선주: 네. 저도 운동을 정말 좋아해요. 그런데 잘 못 해요.
Yes. I really like working out. But, I'm not so good.

인성: 그렇군요. 그럼 우리 다음에 같이 농구 하러 가요. 제가 가르쳐 줄게요.
I see. Then let's go play basketball together next time. I will teach you.

선주: 정말요? 좋아요! 농구 가르쳐 주세요.
Really? Sounds good! Teach me how to play basketball.

인성: 네, 그럼 다음 주 토요일에 같이 농구 할까요?
Ok. Then, shall we play basketball together next Saturday?

선주: 네, 좋아요. 점심 먹은 다음에 농구 해요.
Yes. Sounds good. Let's play basketball after lunch.

Vocabulary

취미
[chwi-mi]
= hobby

뭐
[mwo]
= what

책
[chaek]
= book

읽다
[ik-tta]
= to read

좋아하다
[jo-a-ha-da]
= to like

운동
[un-dong]
= exercise, workout

어떤
[eo-tteon]
= which, what kind of

잘하다
[ja-ra-da]
= to be good at, to do well

농구
[nong-gu]
= basketball

제일
[je-il]
= the best, the most

정말
[jeong-mal]
= really, very

잘 못 하다
[jal mot ha-da]
= to not be good at, to not do well

우리
[u-ri]
= we, us

다음에
[da-eu-me]
= later, next time

같이
[ga-chi]
= together

가다
[ga-da]
= to go

가르쳐 주다
[ga-reu-chyeo ju-da]
= to teach something to someone

좋다
[jo-ta]
= to be good, to like

다음 주
[da-eum ju]
= next week

토요일
[to-yo-il]
= Saturday

점심
[jeom-sim]
= lunch

먹다
[meok-tta]
= to eat

Grammar Points & Exercises

Study the two grammar points used in the dialogue and practice!

A. Suggestion

VERB + -(으)ㄹ까요? = Shall we VERB?

Ex) 하다 + -(으)ㄹ까요? → 할까요? = Shall we do (it)?

1. 읽다 + -(으)ㄹ까요? ⋯⋯> _____ = Shall we read?

2. 먹다 + -(으)ㄹ까요? ⋯⋯> _____ = Shall we eat?

B. After + Gerund

VERB + -(으)ㄴ 다음에 = after VERB-ing

Ex) 먹다 + -(으)ㄴ 다음에 → 먹은 다음에 = after eating

3. 가다 + -(으)ㄴ 다음에 ⋯⋯> _____ = after going

4. 만나다 + -(으)ㄴ 다음에 ⋯⋯> _____ = after meeting

Study the two pronunciation rules used in the dialogue and practice!

A. When a word or syllable ends with ㄺ and is followed by a consonant, only ㄱ is pronounced, not ㄹ.

 ◀)) *Track 96*

Ex) 읽는 → [익는] → [잉는]*

* If you are wondering why 익는 is pronounced 잉는, please refer to page 122.

흙 → [흑]

Write the pronunciations for the following words, just like the above example.

1. 닭 (chicken) ······> [   ]

2. 닭과 (chicken and) ······> [   ]

B. When a syllable ends with ㅌ and is followed by 이, the ㅌ is pronounced as ㅊ. The ㅇ is essentially dropped, and ㅊ joins forces with ㅣ to become "치".

Ex) 같이 → [가치]

Write the pronunciations for the following words, just like the above example.

3. 밭이다 (to be filtered/drained) ······> [   ]

4. 붙이다 (to stick, to attach) ······> [   ]

Korean Only

Can you understand the entire dialogue without a translation? Test yourself!

- Short Dialogue

인성: 선주 씨는 취미가 뭐예요?

선주: 저는 책 읽는 거 좋아해요.

- Long Dialogue

인성: 선주 씨는 취미가 뭐예요?

선주: 저는 책 읽는 거 좋아해요. 인성 씨는 뭐 좋아하세요?

인성: 저는 운동 좋아해요.

선주: 아, 어떤 운동을 잘하세요?

인성: 저는 농구를 제일 잘해요. 선주 씨도 운동 좋아하세요?

선주: 네. 저도 운동을 정말 좋아해요. 그런데 잘 못 해요.

인성: 그렇군요. 그럼 우리 다음에 같이 농구 하러 가요. 제가 가르쳐 줄게요.

선주: 정말요? 좋아요! 농구 가르쳐 주세요.

인성: 네, 그럼 다음 주 토요일에 같이 농구 할까요?

선주: 네, 좋아요. 점심 먹은 다음에 농구 해요.

Answer Key for grammar exercises

1. 읽을까요? *2.* 먹을까요? *3.* 간 다음에 *4.* 만난 다음에

Answer Key for pronunciation exercises

1. 닥 *2.* 닥꽈* *3.* 바치다 *4.* 부치다

* If you are wondering why 과 is pronounced as 꽈, please refer to page 18.

어떤 영화 좋아해요?

What kind of movie do you like?

•

Movie Date

Short Dialogue with Translation

Start with a simple, two-line dialogue first!

 Track 97

정석: **민아 씨, 어떤 영화 좋아해요?**
Min-a, what kind of movie do you like?

민아: **저는 액션 영화 좋아해요.**
I like action movies.

Vocabulary

씨 [ssi]	= *honorific suffix which implies respect toward the person whose name it is attached to*
어떤 [eo-tteon]	= *what kind of, which*
영화 [yeong-hwa]	= *movie*
좋아하다 [jo-a-ha-da]	= *to like*
저 [jeo]	= *I, me*
액션 [aek-ssyeon]	= *action*

Cultural Tip

A typical date in Korea includes going to see a movie, but a movie date can feel different since most people genuinely enjoy seeing a movie. In fact, people love going to the movies so much that the most popular movie of the year will often draw in 10 million or more viewers, which is about a quarter of the Korean population. The price of a ticket will vary as there are multiple options to consider (which theater, 3D, 4D, Standard, Lounge Seating, VIP, etc.), but the average price is about 10,000KRW.

Long Dialogue with Translation

Now challenge yourself with a longer dialogue!

정석: **민아 씨, 어떤 영화 좋아해요?**
Min-a, what kind of movie do you like?

민아: **저는 액션 영화 좋아해요.**
I like action movies.

정석: **저도 액션 영화 정말 좋아해요.**
I really like action movies, too.

민아: **재미있는 액션 영화 하나 개봉했어요. 우리 그거 볼래요?**
An interesting action movie was released. Do you want to watch that?

정석: **네. 좋아요. 그럼 제가 지금 예매할게요.**
Yes. Sounds good. Then, I will reserve the tickets now.

민아: **네. 고마워요.**
Ok, thank you.

정석: **그럼 영화 보기 전에 밥 먹을까요?**
Then, shall we eat before watching the movie?

민아: **네. 뭐 먹을까요? 정석 씨 좋아하는 삼겹살 먹을까요?**
Ok. What shall we eat? Shall we eat pork belly, which you like?

정석: **삼겹살 먹고 싶은데 냄새날 것 같아요.**
I want to eat pork belly, but I think we might smell bad.

민아: **아, 그럼 뭐 먹을까요?**
Oh, then what shall we eat?

정석: **햄버거 어때요?**
How about hamburgers?

민아: **좋아요. 햄버거 먹으러 가요.**
Alright. Let's go eat hamburgers.

(◀)) *Track 99*

Vocabulary

어떤
[eo-tteon]
= what kind of, which

밥
[bap]
= meal

영화
[yeong-hwa]
= movie

먹다
[meok-tta]
= to eat

좋아하다
[jo-a-ha-da]
= to like

뭐
[mwo]
= what

재미있다
[jae-mi-it-tta]
= to be interesting, to be fun

삼겹살
[sam-gyeop-ssal]
= pork belly

하나
[ha-na]
= one

냄새나다
[naem-sae-na-da]
= to smell (lit. smell comes out)

개봉하다
[gae-bong-ha-da]
= to be released

햄버거
[haem-beo-geo]
= hamburger

그거
[geu-geo]
= that, that one

가다
[ga-da]
= to go

보다
[bo-da]
= to see, to watch

지금
[ji-geum]
= now

예매하다
[ye-mae-ha-da]
= to reserve

고맙다
[go-map-tta]
= to be thankful

Grammar Points & Exercises

Study the two grammar points used in the dialogue and practice!

A. Future Tense with "Will"

◀) *Track 101*

VERB + -(으)ㄹ래요? = Will you VERB?

Ex) 보다 + -(으)ㄹ래요? → 볼래요? = Will you see (it)?

1. 예매하다 + -(으)ㄹ래요? ······> _____ = Will you reserve (it)?

2. 먹다 + -(으)ㄹ래요? ······> _____ = Will you eat?

B. Making a Suggestion to Include Self + Verb

VERB + -(으)러 가요. = Let's go VERB.

Ex) 먹다 + -(으)러 가요. → 먹으러 가요. = Let's go eat.

3. 보다 + -(으)러 가요. ······> _____ = Let's go watch.

4. 쇼핑하다 + -(으)러 가요.······> _____ = Let's go shopping.

Study the two pronunciation rules used in the dialogue and practice!

A. When a syllable ends with ㄱ and is followed by a syllable that begins with a vowel, ㄱ becomes part of the following syllable rather than being pronounced distinctly as two different syllables.

Track 102

Ex) 먹을까요 → [머글까요]

Write the pronunciations for the following words, just like the above example.

1. 먹으러 ······> [   ]

2. 먹을래요 ······> [   ]

B. When a syllable ends with ㅂ and is followed by a syllable that begins with ㅅ, the ㅅ is pronounced as ㅆ.

Ex) 삼겹살 → [삼겹쌀]

Write the pronunciations for the following words, just like the above example.

1. 몹시 (very, really) ······> [   ]

2. 집사 (butler, steward) ······> [   ]

Korean Only

Can you understand the entire dialogue without a translation? Test yourself!

- Short Dialogue

정석: 민아 씨, 어떤 영화 좋아해요?

민아: 저는 액션 영화 좋아해요.

- Long Dialogue

정석: 민아 씨, 어떤 영화 좋아해요?

민아: 저는 액션 영화 좋아해요.

정석: 저도 액션 영화 정말 좋아해요.

민아: 재미있는 액션 영화 하나 개봉했어요. 우리 그거 볼래요?

정석: 네. 좋아요. 그럼 제가 지금 예매할게요.

민아: 네. 고마워요.

정석: 그럼 영화 보기 전에 밥 먹을까요?

민아: 네. 뭐 먹을까요? 정석 씨 좋아하는 삼겹살 먹을까요?

정석: 삼겹살 먹고 싶은데 냄새날 것 같아요.

민아: 아, 그럼 뭐 먹을까요?

정석: 햄버거 어때요?

민아: 좋아요. 햄버거 먹으러 가요.

Answer Key for grammar exercises

1. 예매할래요? *2.* 먹을래요? *3.* 보러 가요. *4.* 쇼핑하러 가요.

Answer Key for pronunciation exercises

1. 머그러 *2.* 머글래요 *3.* 몹씨 *4.* 집싸

우리 공원에서 자전거 탈까요?
Shall we ride bicycles in the park?

•

Park

Short Dialogue with Translation

Start with a simple, two-line dialogue first!

 Track 103

민수: **우리 공원에서 자전거 탈까요?**
Shall we ride bicycles in the park?

지연: **저 자전거 없어요.**
I don't have a bike.

Vocabulary

우리 [u-ri]	= *we, us*
공원 [gong-won]	= *park*
-에서 [-e-seo]	= *at, in, from*
자전거 [ja-jeon-geo]	= *bicycle*
타다 [ta-da]	= *to ride*
VERB + -(으)ㄹ까요? [-(eu)l-kka-yo?]	= *Shall we VERB?*
저 [jeo]	= *I, me*
없다 [eop-tta]	= *to not exist, to not have, to not be there*

Cultural Tip

The Han River runs through the middle of Seoul and has twelve riverside parks along its banks. There are bicycle lanes, pedestrian walkways, and a few restaurants in the parks. Many people gather by the Han River when the weather is nice and have a picnic or ride a bike. Bike rentals are plentiful along the Han River, so don't worry if you don't own one!

Long Dialogue with Translation
Now challenge yourself with a longer dialogue!

Track 105

민수: 오늘 날씨 정말 좋네요.
Today's weather is so nice.

지연: 네. 그러네요.
Yes, it is.

민수: 날씨도 좋은데, 우리 공원에서 자전거 탈까요?
Since the weather is nice, shall we ride bicycles in the park?

지연: 저 자전거 없어요.
I don't have a bike.

민수: 한강에서 자전거 빌릴 수 있어요.
You can rent a bike at the Han River.

지연: 아, 그래요? 그런데 저 자전거 못 타요.
Oh, really? But, I can't ride a bike.

민수: 괜찮아요. 제 뒤에 타세요.
It's ok. Ride behind me.

지연: 정말요? 좋아요. 그럼 한강에 가요.
Really? Sounds good. Then, let's go to the Han River.

민수: 자전거 빌리려면, 한 시간쯤 기다려야 돼요.
To rent a bike, we have to wait about an hour.

지연: 그럼 우리 자전거 타기 전에 점심 먹어요.
Then let's eat lunch before we ride bicycles.

민수: 네. 라면 먹을까요?
Ok. Shall we eat ramen?

지연: 좋아요.
Sounds good.

Vocabulary

오늘 [o-neul]	= today	그런데 [geu-reon-de]	= but, however
날씨 [nal-ssi]	= weather	괜찮다 [gwaen-chan-ta]	= to be ok, to be alright
정말 [jeong-mal]	= really, very	뒤 [dwi]	= behind
좋다 [jo-ta]	= to be good, to like	그럼 [geu-reom]	= then
우리 [u-ri]	= we, us	가다 [ga-da]	= to go
공원 [gong-won]	= park	한 시간 [han si-gan]	= one hour
자전거 [ja-jeon-geo]	= bicycle	쯤 [jjeum]	= about, around
타다 [ta-da]	= to ride, to take	기다리다 [gi-da-ri-da]	= to wait
없다 [eop-tta]	= to not exist, to not have, to not be there	점심 [jeom-sim]	= lunch
한강 [han-gang]	= Han River	먹다 [meok-tta]	= to eat
빌리다 [bil-li-da]	= to borrow, to rent	라면 [la-myeon]	= instant noodles, ramen

Grammar Points & Exercises

Study the two grammar points used in the dialogue and practice!

A. Subordinating Conjunction

VERB + -(으)려면 = in order to VERB

 Track 107

Ex) 빌리다 + -(으)려면 → 빌리려면 = in order to rent

1. 타다 + -(으)려면 ······〉 _____ = in order to ride

2. 기다리다 + -(으)려면 ······〉 _____ = in order to wait

B. Before + Gerund

VERB + -기 전에 = before VERB-ing

Ex) 타다 + -기 전에 → 타기 전에 = before riding

3. 빌리다 + -기 전에 ······〉 _____ = before renting

4. 먹다 + -기 전에 ······〉 _____ = before eating

Study the two pronunciation rules used in the dialogue and practice!

A. When a syllable ends with ㅎ and is followed by a syllable that begins with ㄴ, the ㅎ is pronounced as ㄴ.

◀◉) *Track 108*

Ex) 좋네요 → [존네요]

Write the pronunciations for the following words, just like the above example.

1. 놓는 ┈┈⟩ [   ]

2. 쌓네 ┈┈⟩ [   ]

B. When a syllable ends with ㅎ and is followed by a syllable that begins with a vowel, ㅎ is not pronounced.

Ex) 좋아요 → [조아요]

Write the pronunciations for the following words, just like the above example.

3. 놓아요 ┈┈⟩ [   ]

4. 낳아요 ┈┈⟩ [   ]

Korean Only

Can you understand the entire dialogue without a translation? Test yourself!

- **Short Dialogue**

민수: 우리 공원에서 자전거 탈까요?

지연: 저 자전거 없어요.

- **Long Dialogue**

민수: 오늘 날씨 정말 좋네요.

지연: 네. 그러네요.

민수: 날씨도 좋은데, 우리 공원에서 자전거 탈까요?

지연: 저 자전거 없어요.

민수: 한강에서 자전거 빌릴 수 있어요.

지연: 아, 그래요? 그런데 저 자전거 못 타요.

민수: 괜찮아요. 제 뒤에 타세요.

지연: 정말요? 좋아요. 그럼 한강에 가요.

민수: 자전거 빌리려면, 한 시간쯤 기다려야 돼요.

지연: 그럼 우리 자전거 타기 전에 점심 먹어요.

민수: 네. 라면 먹을까요?

지연: 좋아요.

Answer Key for grammar exercises

1. 타려면 *2.* 기다리려면 *3.* 빌리기 전에 *4.* 먹기 전에

Answer Key for pronunciation exercises

1. 논는 *2.* 싼네 *3.* 노아요 *4.* 나아요

나 할 말이 있어.

I have something to tell you.

•

Confessing

Short Dialogue with Translation

Start with a simple, two-line dialogue first!

 Track 109

준호: **미선아, 나 할 말이 있어. 나 너 좋아해.**
Mi-seon, I have something to tell you. I like you.

미선: **정말이야?**
Really?

Vocabulary

할 말 [hal mal]	= *something to say*
있다 [it-tta]	= *to exist, to have*
나 [na]	= *I*
너 [neo]	= *you*
좋아하다 [jo-a-ha-da]	= *to like*
정말 [jeong-mal]	= *really, very*

Cultural Tip

In Korean, if a speaker does not end their sentence with -요, they are using 반말[ban-mal], or casual language. Children use 반말 when talking to each other, but adults rarely use 반말 unless they have a close and casual relationship with one another.

Long Dialogue with Translation

Now challenge yourself with a longer dialogue!

Track 111

준호: **미선아, 지금 시간 있어?**
Mi-seon, do you have some time right now (to talk)?

미선: **왜?**
Why?

준호: **나 할 말이 있어.**
I have something to tell you.

미선: **뭔데?**
What is it?

준호: **나 너 좋아해.**
I like you.

미선: **장난치지 마.**
Don't mess with me.

준호: **장난 아니야. 진심이야. 친구 말고 남자 친구 하고 싶어.**
I'm not kidding. I mean it. I want to be your boyfriend instead of a friend.

미선: **정말이야?**
Really?

준호: **응. 너 처음 봤을 때부터 좋아했어.**
Yes. I've liked you since the first time that I saw you.

미선: **정말 몰랐어.**
I really didn't know.

준호: **너는 나 어때?**
What do you think about me?

미선: **사실 나도 너 좋아하고 있었어.**
Actually, I've liked you too.

준호: **정말? 고마워.**
Really? Thank you.

Vocabulary

지금
[ji-geum]
= *now*

처음
[cheo-eum]
= *first*

시간
[si-gan]
= *time*

보다
[bo-da]
= *to see, to watch*

있다
[it-tta]
= *to exist, to have*

모르다
[mo-reu-da]
= *to not know*

왜
[wae]
= *why*

사실
[sa-sil]
= *actually*

할 말
[hal mal]
= *something to say*

고맙다
[go-map-tta]
= *to be thankful*

좋아하다
[jo-a-ha-da]
= *to like*

장난치다
[jang-nan-chi-da]
= *to mess with someone*

진심
[jin-sim]
= *sincerity, honest feeling*

친구
[chin-gu]
= *friend*

남자 친구
[nam-ja chin-gu]
= *boyfriend*

정말
[jeong-mal]
= *really, very*

Grammar Points & Exercises

Study the two grammar points used in the dialogue and practice!

A. Pair: Not _____, but _____

Track 113

NOUN + 말고 + NOUN = not NOUN, but NOUN

Ex) 친구 + 말고 + 남자 친구 → 친구 말고 남자 친구 = not a friend, but a boyfriend

1. 너 + 말고 + 네 친구 ……〉 _____ = not you, but your friend

2. 그것 + 말고 + 저것 ……〉 _____ = not that one, but that one over there

B. Conjunction: "Since" In Past Tense

VERB/ADJECTIVE + -았/었/였을 때부터
= since the time (SUBJECT) VERB/ADJECTIVE

Ex) 처음 보다 + -았/었/였을 때부터 → 처음 봤을 때부터 = since the first time I saw (them)

3. 어리다 + -았/었/였을 때부터 ……〉 _____ = since I was little/young

4. 만나다 + -았/었/였을 때부터 ……〉 _____ = since the time I met (them)

Pronunciation Points & Exercises

Study the two pronunciation rules used in the dialogue and practice!

A. When a syllable ends with ㅍ and is followed by a syllable that begins with a vowel, ㅍ becomes part of the following syllable rather than being pronounced distinctly as two different syllables.

) *Track 114*

Ex) 싶어 → [시퍼]

Write the pronunciations for the following words, just like the above example.

1. 깊어 ·····> [   ]

2. 짚어 ·····> [   ]

B. When a syllable ends with ㅆ and is followed by a syllable that begins with a vowel, ㅆ becomes part of the following syllable rather than being pronounced distinctly as two different syllables.

Ex) 있어 → [이써]

Write the pronunciations for the following words, just like the above example.

3. 갔어 ·····> [   ]

4. 봤어 ·····> [   ]

Korean Only

Can you understand the entire dialogue without a translation? Test yourself!

- *Short Dialogue*

준호: 미선아, 나 할 말이 있어. 나 너 좋아해.

미선: 정말이야?

- *Long Dialogue*

준호: 미선아, 지금 시간 있어?

미선: 왜?

준호: 나 할 말이 있어.

미선: 뭔데?

준호: 나 너 좋아해.

미선: 장난치지 마.

준호: 장난 아니야. 진심이야. 친구 말고 남자 친구 하고 싶어.

미선: 정말이야?

준호: 응. 너 처음 봤을 때부터 좋아했어.

미선: 정말 몰랐어.

준호: 너는 나 어때?

미선: 사실 나도 너 좋아하고 있었어.

준호: 정말? 고마워.

Answer Key for grammar exercises

1. 너 말고 네 친구 *2.* 그것 말고 저것 *3.* 어렸을 때부터 *4.* 만났을 때부터

Answer Key for pronunciation exercises

1. 기퍼 *2.* 지퍼 *3.* 가써 *4.* 봐써

Dialogue 20

사귀기 싫어요.
I don't want to date you.

•

Rejection

Real-Life Korean Conversations For Beginners

Short Dialogue with Translation

Start with a simple, two-line dialogue first!

 Track 115

준서: **주희 씨, 남자 친구 있어요?**
Ju-hee, do you have a boyfriend?

주희: **아니요. 없어요.**
No, I don't.

Vocabulary

씨 [ssi]	= *honorific suffix which implies respect toward the person whose name it is attached to*
남자 친구 [nam-ja chin-gu]	= *boyfriend*
있다 [it-ta]	= *to exist, to have*
아니요. [a-ni-yo.]	= *No.*
없다 [eop-tta]	= *to not exist, to not have, to not be there*

Cultural Tip

The native Korean word, 사귀다 [sa-gwi-da], commonly translates as "to go out" or "to date" in English. However, there are also the loanwords 데이트 [de-i-teu], which means "a date", and 데이트하다, meaning "to go on a date". Although these three words seem to be interchangeable, they are definitely used in specific situations to imply different things. 데이트 or 데이트하다 are used when two people are meeting one-on-one or are not officially a couple, while 사귀다 is used to indicate that two people are a couple and have gone out on dates before.

Long Dialogue with Translation
Now challenge yourself with a longer dialogue!

준서: **주희 씨, 남자 친구 있어요?**
Ju-hee, do you have a boyfriend?

◀)) Track 117

주희: **아니요. 없어요.**
No, I don't.

준서: **그래요? 그럼 저는 어때요?**
Really? Well, how about me?

주희: **네? 무슨 말이에요?**
What? What are you talking about?

준서: **저 주희 씨 좋아해요. 주희 씨랑 만나고 싶어요.**
Ju-hee, I like you. I want to go out with you.

주희: **네? 우리 아직 한 번밖에 안 만났어요.**
What? We've only met once so far.

준서: **알아요. 그래도 전 주희 씨가 너무 좋아요. 주희 씨는 제가 싫어요?**
I know. But still, I like you very much, Ju-hee. Do you not like me?

주희: **아니요. 싫지 않아요.**
No, I don't dislike you.

준서: **그럼 우리 사귀어요.**
Then, let's see each other.

주희: **저는 아직 준서 씨 잘 몰라요.**
Jun-seo, I don't know you that well yet.

준서: **천천히 알게 될 거예요.**
You will slowly get to know me.

주희: **아니요. 저는 아직 사귀기 싫어요.**
No, I don't want to date you yet.

Vocabulary

남자 친구 [nam-ja chin-gu]	= boyfriend	싫다 [sil-ta]	= to not like, to hate
있다 [it-ta]	= to exist, to have	그럼 [geu-reom]	= then
없다 [eop-tta]	= to not exist, to not have, to not be there	우리 [u-ri]	= we, us
저 [jeo]	= I, me	사귀다 [sa-gwi-da]	= to date, to go out
무슨 [mu-seun]	= what	잘 [jal]	= well
말 [mal]	= word, talking	모르다 [mo-reu-da]	= to not know
좋아하다 [jo-a-ha-da]	= to like	천천히 [cheon-cheo-ni]	= slowly
만나다 [man-na-da]	= to meet	아직 [a-jik]	= yet
한 번 [han beon]	= once		
알다 [al-da]	= to know		
너무 [neo-mu]	= really, so, too much		

Grammar Points & Exercises

Study the two grammar points used in the dialogue and practice!

A. Making a Suggestion to Include Yourself

우리 + VERB + -아/어/여요. = Let's VERB.

    Ex) 우리 + 사귀다 + -아/어/여요 → 우리 사귀어요. = Let's go out. / Let's date.

    1. 우리 + 만나다 + -아/어/여요 ·······⟩ _____ = Let's meet.

    2. 우리 + 가다 + -아/어/여요 ·······⟩ _____ = Let's go.

B. To Not Like/Want To Do Something

VERB + -기 싫어요. = I don't like VERB-ing, I don't want to VERB.

    Ex) 사귀다 + -기 싫어요. → 사귀기 싫어요. = I don't want to go out (with you).

    3. 하다 + -기 싫어요. ·······⟩ _____ = I don't want to do (it).

    4. 만나다 + -기 싫어요. ·······⟩ _____ = I don't want to meet.

Study the two pronunciation rules used in the dialogue and practice!

A. When a syllable ends with ㅀ and is followed by a syllable that begins with a vowel, only the ㄹ is pronounced while ㅎ is not pronounced.

Ex) 싫어요 → [시러요]

* If you are wondering why 실어 is pronounced 시러, please refer to page 18.

B. When a syllable ends with ㅀ and is followed by a syllable that begins with ㅈ, the ㄹ is pronounced, but the ㅎ changes the pronunciation of ㅈ to ㅊ. ㅎ is not pronounced because it is used to create the ㅊ sound.

Ex) 싫지 → [실치]

Write the pronunciations for the following words, just like the above example.

1. 닳아요 ······> [   ]

2. 닳지 ······> [   ]

Can you understand the entire dialogue without a translation? Test yourself!

- Short Dialogue

준서: 주희 씨, 남자 친구 있어요?

주희: 아니요. 없어요.

- Long Dialogue

준서: 주희 씨, 남자 친구 있어요?

주희: 아니요. 없어요.

준서: 그래요? 그럼 저는 어때요?

주희: 네? 무슨 말이에요?

준서: 저 주희 씨 좋아해요. 주희 씨랑 만나고 싶어요.

주희: 네? 우리 아직 한 번밖에 안 만났어요.

준서: 알아요. 그래도 전 주희 씨가 너무 좋아요. 주희 씨는 제가 싫어요?

주희: 아니요. 싫지 않아요.

준서: 그럼 우리 사귀어요.

주희: 저는 아직 준서 씨 잘 몰라요.

준서: 천천히 알게 될 거예요.

주희: 아니요. 저는 아직 사귀기 싫어요.

Answer Key for grammar exercises

1. 우리 만나요. 2. 우리 가요. 3. 하기 싫어요. 4. 만나기 싫어요.

Answer Key for pronunciation exercises

1. 다라요 2. 달치

Dialogue 21

또 야근해요?
Are you working overtime again?

•

Overtime Work

Real-Life Korean Conversations For Beginners

Short Dialogue with Translation

Start with a simple, two-line dialogue first!

미화: **또 야근해요?**
Are you working overtime again?

성일: **네. 오늘 야근해야 돼요.**
Yes. I have to work overtime today.

Vocabulary

또
[tto]

= *again*

야근하다
[ya-geu-na-da]

= *to work overtime*

네.
[ne.]

= *Yes. / Ok.*

오늘
[o-neul]

= *today*

VERB + -아/어/여야 돼요.
[-a/eo/yeo-ya dwae-yo.]

= *I have to VERB.*

Cultural Tip

With the exception of civil servants and those who work for foreign-based companies, workers in Korea often must work overtime. In addition to overtime, the office culture in some companies can even affect your personal schedule; you are not allowed to leave before your boss leaves, and it is proper etiquette to show up before your boss arrives.

Long Dialogue with Translation

Now challenge yourself with a longer dialogue!

◀)) *Track 123*

(On the phone)

미화: 여보, 오늘 언제 와요?
Honey, what time are you
coming home today?

성일: 오늘 늦을 거예요.
I will come late today.

미화: 또 야근해요?
Are you working overtime
again?

성일: 네.
Yeah.

미화: 아휴.
Phew.

성일: 왜요?
Why?

미화: 오늘은 일찍 와요. 네?
Come early today, will
you?

성일: 왜요?
Why?

미화: 진짜 몰라요?
You really don't know?

성일: 네. 몰라요.
Yeah. I don't know.

미화: 오늘 우리 결혼기념일이에요.
Today is our wedding
anniversary.

성일: 네? 오늘이 며칠이에요?
What? What's today's date?

미화: 2월 23일이요.
It's February 23.

성일: 우리 결혼기념일은 2월 25일
이에요.
Our wedding anniversary is
February 25.

미화: 네? 아··· 미안해요.
Huh? Oh... I'm sorry.

성일: 오늘 야근해야 돼요. 25일에는
일찍 갈게요.
I have to work overtime today. I
will go home early on the 25th.

미화: 네.
Ok.

Vocabulary

여보 [yeo-bo]	= honey (between a married couple)	**결혼기념일** [gyeo-ron-gi-nyeo-mil]	= wedding anniversary
오늘 [o-neul]	= today	**며칠** [myeo-chil]	= what date
늦다 [neut-tta]	= to be late	**미안하다** [mi-a-na-da]	= to be sorry
또 [tto]	= again		
야근하다 [ya-geu-na-da]	= to work overtime		
왜 [wae]	= why		
일찍 [il-jjik]	= early		
오다 [o-da]	= to come		
진짜 [jin-jja]	= really		
모르다 [mo-reu-da]	= to not know		
우리 [u-ri]	= we, us		

Grammar Points & Exercises
Study the two grammar points used in the dialogue and practice!

A. Future Tense

VERB + -(으)ㄹ 거예요. = I am going to VERB.

Ex) 늦다 + -(으)ㄹ 거예요 → 늦을 거예요. = I am going to be late.

1. 야근하다 + -(으)ㄹ 거예요 ······〉 _____ = I am going to work overtime.

2. 오다 + -(으)ㄹ 거예요 ······〉 _____ = I am going to come.

B. Obligation

VERB + -아/어/여야 돼요. = I have to VERB.

Ex) 야근하다 + -아/어/여야 돼요 → 야근해야 돼요. = I have to work overtime.

3. 오다 + -아/어/여야 돼요 ······〉 _____ = I have to come.

4. 웃다 + -아/어/여야 돼요 ······〉 _____ = I have to smile.

Study the two pronunciation rules used in the dialogue and practice!

A. When a syllable ends with ㅈ and is followed by a syllable that
begins with a vowel, ㅈ becomes part of the following syllable rather
than being pronounced distinctly as two different syllables.

Ex) 늦을 → [느즐]

Write the pronunciations for the following words, just like the above example.

1. 늦어 ······> [   ]

2. 짖으면 ······> [   ]

B. When a syllable ends with ㄴ and is followed by a syllable that begins with ㅎ, ㄴ
becomes part of the following syllable and ㅎ is not pronounced.
* Not an official pronunciation rule, but it is done for easier pronunciation.

Ex) 번호 → [버노]

Write the pronunciations for the following words, just like the above example.

3. 전화 (phone call) ······> [   ]

4. 분홍색 (pink color) ······> [   ]

Korean Only

Can you understand the entire dialogue without a translation? Test yourself!

- Short Dialogue

미화: 또 야근해요?

성일: 네. 오늘 야근해야 돼요.

- Long Dialogue

미화: 여보, 오늘 언제 와요?

성일: 오늘 늦을 거예요.

미화: 또 야근해요?

성일: 네.

미화: 아휴.

성일: 왜요?

미화: 오늘은 일찍 와요. 네?

성일: 왜요?

미화: 진짜 몰라요?

성일: 네. 몰라요.

미화: 오늘 우리 결혼기념일이에요.

성일: 네? 오늘이 며칠이에요?

미화: 2월 23일이요.

성일: 우리 결혼기념일은 2월 25일이에요.

미화: 네? 아… 미안해요.

성일: 오늘 야근해야 돼요. 25일에는 일찍 갈게요.

미화: 네.

Answer Key for grammar exercises

1. 야근할 거예요. *2.* 올 거예요. *3.* 와야 돼요. *4.* 웃어야 돼요.

Answer Key for pronunciation exercises

1. 느저 *2.* 지즈면 *3.* 저놔 *4.* 부농색

5분 후에 회의 시작해.

The meeting starts in 5 minutes.

•

Meeting

Short Dialogue with Translation

Start with a simple, two-line dialogue first!

 Track 127

최 대리: **오늘 회의 준비 다 했어?**
Have you finished preparing for the meeting today?

선 대리: **아니, 아직 못 했어.**
No, I haven't.

Vocabulary

오늘 [o-neul]	= today	**아니** [a-ni]	= no (casual)
회의 [hoe-ui]	= meeting	**아직** [a-jik]	= yet
준비 [jun-bi]	= preparation	**다 하다** [da ha-da]	= to be finished, to be all done
못 VERB + **-았/었/였어.** [mot] -a/eo/yeo-sseo.]	= I couldn't VERB. (casual)		

Cultural Tip

In many Korean companies, your rank or position within the company determines how you address your colleagues. If you are in a lower position/rank than the person with whom you are speaking, you must attach the honorific suffix - 님 [-nim] to the person's title. Even if you are in a higher position than the person you are addressing, if you are younger than him/her, you may also need to use -님. For example, if you need to talk with someone who is a "section chief" (과장 [gwa-jang]) you should address that person as 과장님. If there are many people who have the title of 과장, you must use their family name + 과장 +님 to make it clear to whom you are speaking.

Example:
최 과장님 = Choi (family name) + Section Chief + - 님
김 부장님 = Kim (family name) + Team Leader* + -님
박 팀장님 = Pak (family name)** + Team Manager*** + -님

Native Korean word for "team leader"

** 박 *is most commonly spelled and pronounced as "Park" in English, but when speaking Korean, it is [pak].*

*** 팀 *in* 팀장 *[tim-jang] is borrowed from the English word "team".*

Long Dialogue with Translation

Now challenge yourself with a longer dialogue!

최 대리: **오늘 회의 준비 다 했어?**
Have you finished preparing for the meeting today?

Track 129

선 대리: **아니, 아직 못 했어.**
No, I haven't.

최 대리: **진짜? 5분 후에 회의 시작해.**
Really?

선 대리: **금방 해.**
I will be done soon.

최 대리: **과장님 지금 회의실 간다.**
The section chief is going to the meeting room now.

선 대리: **너 먼저 가. 나 금방 갈게.**
You go first. I will be there soon.

최 대리: **알았어.**
Ok.

(Later)

최 대리: **선 대리, 천천히 해.**
Take your time.

선 대리: **왜? 과장님 화났어?**
Why? Is the section chief mad?

최 대리: **아니. 과장님 아파서 병원 가셨어.**
No. The section chief is sick, so he went to the hospital.

선 대리: **진짜? 그럼 회의는?**
Really? Then what about the meeting?

최 대리: **회의는 내일 할 거야.**
We'll have the meeting tomorrow.

Vocabulary

오늘 [o-neul]	= today	먼저 [meon-jeo]	= first, earlier
회의 [hoe-ui]	= meeting	가다 [ga-da]	= to go
준비 [jun-bi]	= preparation	알다 [al-da]	= to know
다 하다 [da ha-da]	= to be finished, to be all done	대리 [dae-ri]	– assistant manager
아직 [a-jik]	= yet	천천히 [cheon-cheo-ni]	= slowly
진짜 [jin-jja]	= really	하다 [ha-da]	= to do
후 [hu]	= after	화나다 [hwa-na-da]	= to be angry
시작하다 [si-ja-ka-da]	= to start	왜 [wae]	= why
금방 [geum-bang]	= soon	아프다 [a-peu-da]	= to be sick
과장님 [gwa-jang-nim]	= section chief	병원 [byeong-won]	= hospital, doctor's office
회의실 [hoe-ui-sil]	= meeting room	내일 [nae-il]	= tomorrow

Grammar Points & Exercises

Study the two grammar points used in the dialogue and practice!

A. Narrative Present Tense

◀◐) Track 131

VERB + -ㄴ/는다!

= (SUBJECT) is VERB-ing! / (SUBJECT) is about to VERB!

* If the verb stem ends with a vowel, it is followed by -ㄴ다. If the verb stem ends with a consonant, it is followed by -는다. If a verb stem ends with ㄹ, drop the ㄹ and add -ㄴ다.

** This ending is used to show surprise or discovery of a certain fact.

Ex) 과장님 회의실 + 가다 + -ㄴ/는다

→ 과장님 회의실 간다. = The section chief is going to the meeting room!

1. 시작하다 + -ㄴ/는다! ……〉 _____ = It is about to start!

2. 오다 + -ㄴ/는다! ……〉 _____ = (They) are coming!

B. Casual Future Tense

VERB + -(으)ㄹ 거야 = I am going to VERB.

Ex) 하다 + -(으)ㄹ 거야 → 할 거야. = I am going to do (it).

3. 가다 + -(으)ㄹ 거야 ……〉 _____ = I am going to go.

4. 보다 + -(으)ㄹ 거야 ……〉 _____ = I am going to see.

Study the two pronunciation rules used in the dialogue and practice!

A. 의 can be pronounced as 이 EXCEPT when 의 is the first syllable of a word.

◀)) *Track 132*

    Ex) 회의 → [회의] or [회이]

Write the pronunciations for the following words, just like the above example.

    1. 논의 (discussion, debate) ······> [   ] or [   ]

    2. 주의 (attention, caution) ······> [   ] or [   ]

B. Take a moment to review some pronunciation rules that were previously covered.

Write the pronunciations for the following phrases from the dialogue.

    3. 했어 ······> [   ]

    4. 시작해 ······> [   ]

    5. 갈게 ······> [   ]

    6. 천천히 ······> [   ]

Korean Only

Can you understand the entire dialogue without a translation? Test yourself!

- Short Dialogue

최 대리: 오늘 회의 준비 다 했어?

선 대리: 아니, 아직 못 했어.

- Long Dialogue

최 대리: 오늘 회의 준비 다 했어?

선 대리: 아니, 아직 못 했어.

최 대리: 진짜? 5분 후에 회의 시작해.

선 대리: 금방 해.

최 대리: 과장님 지금 회의실 간다.

선 대리: 너 먼저 가. 나 금방 갈게.

최 대리: 알았어.

최 대리: 선 대리, 천천히 해.

선 대리: 왜? 과장님 화났어?

최 대리: 아니. 과장님 아파서 병원 가셨어.

선 대리: 진짜? 그럼 회의는?

최 대리: 회의는 내일 할 거야.

Answer Key for grammar exercises

1. 시작한다! *2.* 온다! *3.* 갈 거야. *4.* 볼 거야.

Answer Key for pronunciation exercises

1. 노늬, 노니 *2.* 주의, 주이 *3.* 해써 *4.* 시자캐 *5.* 갈께 *6.* 천처니

이메일 확인했어?
Did you check your e-mail?

•

Work Schedule

Short Dialogue with Translation
Start with a simple, two-line dialogue first!

 Track 133

팀장: 김 대리, 이메일 확인했어?
Mr. Kim, did you check your e-mail?

김 대리: 네? 아니요. 지금 할게요.
Huh? No. I will check it now.

Vocabulary

대리 [dae-ri]	= *assistant manager*
이메일 [i-me-il]	= *e-mail*
확인하다 [hwa-gi-na-da]	= *to check*
네? [ne?]	= *Huh? / Sorry? / Pardon?*
아니요. [a-ni-yo.]	= *No.*
지금 [ji-geum]	= *now*
하다 [ha-da]	= *to do*
VERB + -(으)ㄹ게요. [-(eu)l-kke-yo.]	= *I will VERB.*

Cultural Tip

Some older Korean companies use military-style leadership to manage their employees. People who work in these types of companies are expected to listen to whatever the boss says and "take orders" without question. This often leads to personal obligations being ignored, such as spending time with family or friends. There is rarely an opportunity or prior obligation that warrants ignoring a boss' suggestion.

Long Dialogue with Translation

Now challenge yourself with a longer dialogue!

○ 팀장: 김 대리, 이메일 확인했어?
　　Mr. Kim, did you check your e-mail?

Track 135

○ 김 대리: 네? 아니요. 지금 할게요.
　　Huh? No. I will check it now.

○ 팀장: 우리 일본 출장 가야 돼.
　　We have to go on a business trip to Japan.

○ 김 대리: 진짜요? 언제요?
　　Really? When?

○ 팀장: 오늘.
　　Today.

○ 김 대리: 네? 오늘이요?
　　Huh? Today?

○ 팀장: 그래, 오늘. 아휴.
　　Yes, today. (Sigh)

○ 김 대리: 그럼 오늘 회의는요?
　　Then, what about today's meeting?

○ 팀장: 취소야.
　　It's cancelled.

○ 김 대리: 과장님, 저 이 옷밖에 없어요.
　　Sir, I only have these clothes.

○ 팀장: 나도 이 옷밖에 없어. 가기 전에 셔츠 하나 사자.
　　I too only have these clothes. Let's buy a shirt before we go.

○ 김 대리: 네, 알겠습니다.
　　Ok, I understand.

Vocabulary

대리 [dae-ri]	= *assistant manager*	오늘 [o-neul]	= *today*
이메일 [i-me-il]	= *e-mail*	아휴 [a-hyu]	= *onomatopoeia for a sigh in Korean*
확인하다 [hwa-gi-na-da]	= *to check*	그럼 [geu-reom]	= *then*
지금 [ji-geum]	= *now*	회의 [hoe-ui]	= *meeting*
하다 [ha-da]	= *to do*	취소 [chwi-so]	= *cancellation*
우리 [u-ri]	= *we, us*	옷 [ot]	= *clothes*
일본 [il-bon]	= *Japan*	없다 [eop-tta]	= *to not exist, to not have, to not be there*
출장 [chul-jjang]	= *business trip*	가다 [ga-da]	= *to go*
가다 [ga-da]	= *to go*	전 [jeon]	= *before*
진짜 [jin-jja]	= *really*	하나 [ha-na]	= *one*
언제 [eon-je]	= *when*	사다 [sa-da]	= *to buy*

Grammar Points & Exercises

Study the two grammar points used in the dialogue and practice!

A. Past Interrogative Sentence

Track 137

VERB + -았/었/였어(요)? = Did (subject) VERB?

Ex) 확인하다 + -았/었/였어(요)? → 확인했어(요)? = Did you check?

1. 가다 + -았/었/였어(요)? ……⟩ _____ = Did you go?

2. 사다 + -았/었/였어(요)? ……⟩ _____ = Did you buy (it)?

B. Adjective: "Only" or "Nothing but"

NOUN + -밖에 없어요.

= There is nothing but NOUN. / There is only NOUN.

Ex) 이 옷 + -밖에 없어요 → 이 옷밖에 없어요.

= There's nothing but these clothes. / I only have these clothes.

3. 오늘 + -밖에 없어요 ……⟩ _____ = There's nothing but today.

4. 하나 + -밖에 없어요 ……⟩ _____ = There's only one.

Pronunciation Points & Exercises

Study the two pronunciation rules used in the dialogue and practice!

A. For Sino-Korean words (words influenced by hanja or Chinese characters), when a syllable ends with ㄹ and is followed by a syllable that begins with ㅈ, ㅈ is pronounced as ㅉ.

◀0) *Track 138*

Ex) 출장 → [출짱]

Write the pronunciations for the following words, just like the above example.

1. 발전 (development) ·····> [   ]

2. 물질 (matter, substance) ·····> [   ]

B. When a syllable ends with ㅅ (which sounds the same as ㄷ when in the 받침 position) and is followed by a syllable that begins with ㅂ, the ㅂ is pronounced as ㅃ.

Ex) 옷밖에 → [옫빠께]

* If you are wondering why 빡에 is pronounced as 빠께, please refer to page 106.

Write the pronunciations for the following words, just like the above example.

3. 못밖에 ·····> [   ]

4. 붓밖에 ·····> [   ]

Korean Only

Can you understand the entire dialogue without a translation? Test yourself!

- Short Dialogue

팀장: 김 대리, 이메일 확인했어?

김 대리: 네? 아니요. 지금 할게요.

- Long Dialogue

팀장: 김 대리, 이메일 확인했어?

김 대리: 네? 아니요. 지금 할게요.

팀장: 우리 일본 출장 가야 돼.

김 대리: 진짜요? 언제요?

팀장: 오늘.

김 대리: 네? 오늘이요?

팀장: 그래, 오늘. 아휴.

김 대리: 그럼 오늘 회의는요?

팀장: 취소야.

김 대리: 과장님, 저 이 옷밖에 없어요.

팀장: 나도 이 옷밖에 없어. 가기 전에 셔츠 하나 사자.

김 대리: 네, 알겠습니다.

Answer Key for grammar exercises

1. 갔어요? *2.* 샀어요? *3.* 오늘밖에 없어요. *4.* 하나밖에 없어요.

Answer Key for pronunciation exercises

1. 발쩐 *2.* 물찔 *3.* 몯빠께 *4.* 붇빠께

취업 축하해요!
Congratulations on getting a job!

•

Getting a Job

Start with a simple, two-line dialogue first!

Track 139

선미: **선배! 취업 축하해요!**
Congratulations on getting a job!

선배: **고마워.**
Thank you.

Vocabulary

선배
[seon-bae]
= senior

취업
[chwi-eop]
= getting a job

축하하다
[chu-ka-ha-da]
= to congratulate, to celebrate

고맙다
[go-map-tta]
= to be thankful

Cultural Tip

The word 선배 [seon-bae] is used to address someone who joined an organization (school, job, club, etc.) earlier than you. A person who joined an organization after you, or after the 선배, is called 후배 [hu-bae]. The 선배-후배 culture creates a strong hierarchy in addition to "age hierarchy". In a formal setting, even if a younger person happens to be 선배, the older 후배 must use polite language when speaking to their 선배.

Long Dialogue with Translation

Now challenge yourself with a longer dialogue!

◀)) *Track 141*

선미: **선배! 취업 축하해요.**
Congratulations on getting a job!

선배: **고마워. 너는?**
Thank you. What about you?

선미: **취업 너무 힘들어요.**
Getting a job is so hard.

선배: **이력서 냈어?**
Did you submit your résumé?

선미: **네. 진짜 많이 냈어요.**
Yes. I've submitted it to so many places.

선배: **한 군데도 연락 안 왔어?**
You haven't heard from any?

선미: **네. 선배, 저 술 사 주세요.**
Yeah. Please buy me a drink.

선배: **그래. 술 마시자.**
Ok. Let's drink.

선미: **고기도 사 주세요.**
Please buy me some meat, too.

선배: **고기? 나 아직 백수야. 돈 없어.**
Meat? I am still jobless. I don't have money.

선미: **저는 한 군데도 연락 안 왔어요. 슬퍼요.**
I haven't heard back from a single place. I'm sad.

선배: **알았어. 고기 먹자. 그리고 술도 마시자.**
Ok. Let's eat meat. And let's drink, too.

선미: **네! 좋아요!**
Ok! Sounds good!

Vocabulary

선배
[seon-bae]
= senior

술
[sul]
= alcoholic drink

취업
[chwi-eop]
= getting a job

사 주다
[sa ju-da]
= to buy someone something

축하하다
[chu-ka-ha-da]
= to congratulate, to celebrate

그래
[geu-rae]
= ok (casual)

고맙다
[go-map-tta]
= to be thankful

마시다
[ma-si-da]
= to drink

너무
[neo-mu]
= really, so, too much

고기
[go-gi]
= meat

힘들다
[him-deul-da]
= to be tough, to be difficult, to be hard

아직
[a-jik]
= yet

이력서
[i-ryeok-sseo]
= résumé

백수
[baek-ssu]
= jobless

내다
[nae-da]
= to submit

돈
[don]
= money

진짜
[jin-jja]
= really

없다
[eop-tta]
= to not exist, to not have, to not be there

많이
[ma-ni]
= many, much, a lot

슬프다
[seul-peu-da]
= to be sad

한 군데
[han gun-de]
= one place

먹다
[meok-tta]
= to eat

연락
[yeol-lak]
= contact

좋다
[jo-ta]
= to be good, to like

오다
[o-da]
= to come

Grammar Points & Exercises

Study the two grammar points used in the dialogue and practice!

A. Past Tense Sentence

VERB + -았/었/였어요. = (SUBJECT) VERB-ed.

Ex) 내다 + -았/었였어요 → 냈어요. = (They) submitted.

1. 하다 + -았/었/였어요 ······⟩ _____ = (They) did.

2. 가다 + -았/었/였어요 ······⟩ _____ = (They) went.

B. Negative Past Tense Sentence

안 + VERB + -았/었/였어요. = (SUBJECT) did not VERB.

Ex) 안 + 오다 + -았/었/였어요. → 안 왔어요. = (They) did not come.

3. 안 + 내다 + -았/었/였어요 ······⟩ _____ = (They) didn't submit.

4. 안 + 먹다 + -았/었/였어요 ······⟩ _____ = (They) didn't eat.

Study the two pronunciation rules used in the dialogue and practice!

A. When a syllable ends with ㄱ and is followed by a syllable that begins with ㅅ, the ㅅ is pronounced as ㅆ.

◀) **Track 144**

   Ex) 이력서 → [이력써]

Write the pronunciations for the following words, just like the above example.

   1. 백수 (jobless) ·····〉 [   ]

   2. 박수 (applause, clapping) ·····〉 [   ]

B. When a syllable ends with ㄱ and is followed by a syllable that begins with ㅈ, the ㅈ is pronounced as ㅉ.

   Ex) 먹자 → [먹짜]

Write the pronunciations for the following words, just like the above example.

   3. 국자 (ladle) ·····〉 [   ]

   4. 직장 (job, workplace) ·····〉 [   ]

Korean Only
Can you understand the entire dialogue without a translation? Test yourself!

- Short Dialogue

선미: 선배! 취업 축하해요!

선배: 고마워.

- Long Dialogue

선미: 선배! 취업 축하해요.

선배: 고마워. 너는?

선미: 취업 너무 힘들어요.

선배: 이력서 냈어?

선미: 네. 진짜 많이 냈어요.

선배: 한 군데도 연락 안 왔어?

선미: 네. 선배, 저 술 사 주세요.

선배: 그래. 술 마시자.

선미: 고기도 사 주세요.

선배: 고기? 나 아직 백수야. 돈 없어.

선미: 저는 한 군데도 연락 안 왔어요. 슬퍼요.

선배: 알았어. 고기 먹자. 그리고 술도 마시자.

선미: 네! 좋아요!

Answer Key for grammar exercises

1. 했어요. *2.* 갔어요. *3.* 안 냈어요. *4.* 안 먹었어요.

Answer Key for pronunciation exercises

1. 백쑤 *2.* 박쑤 *3.* 국짜 *4.* 직짱

Dialogue 25

저 안 취했어요.
I am not drunk.

•

Company Dinner

Short Dialogue with Translation
Start with a simple, two-line dialogue first!

Track 145

팀장: **선미 씨, 취했어?**
Seon-mi, are you drunk?

선미: **아니요. 저 안 취했어요.**
No. I am not drunk.

Vocabulary

취하다 [chwi-ha-da]	= *to be drunk*
아니요. [a-ni-yo.]	= *No.*
저 [jeo]	= *I, me*
안 VERB + -았/었/였어요. [an -a/eo/yeo-sseo-yo.]	= *(SUBJECT) didn't VERB.*

Cultural Tip

회식 [hoe-sik], or "company dinner", is when a group of employees go out for dinner after work. 회식 is typically considered part of the job even though it is after work hours, and employees should not turn down an invitation to 회식 due to personal plans. Employees are also often encouraged by the boss to consume copious amounts of alcohol. However, these days there are some managers who are trying to change the 회식 culture by having it less often, or having only dinner and no drinks.

Long Dialogue with Translation
Now challenge yourself with a longer dialogue!

◀》 *Track 147*

선미: **팀장님! 건배!**
Boss! Cheers!

팀장: **선미 씨, 취했어?**
Seon-mi, are you drunk?

선미: **아니요! 저 안 취했어요.**
No! I am not drunk.

팀장: **선미 씨 지금 엄청 취했어.**
You are very drunk now.

선미: **아니요. 저 안 취했어요. 팀장님, 감사합니다.**
No, I am not drunk. Thank you, boss.

팀장: **왜?**
Why?

선미: **저 조금밖에 안 마셨어요. 팀장님! 감사합니다!**
I've only had a little bit to drink. Thank you, boss!

팀장: **아이고, 많이 취했네.**
Oh my god. You are really drunk.

선미: **감사합니다! 저 취업하는 거 힘들었어요. 감사합니다.**
Thank you! Getting a job was so hard. Thank you.

팀장: **자, 택시비. 택시 타고 빨리 들어가.**
Here is some taxi fare for you. Get a taxi and go home quickly.

선미: **우와! 감사합니다, 팀장님. 감사합니다.**
저 안 취했어요.
Wow! Thank you. Thank you, boss.
I am not drunk.

Vocabulary

건배
[geon-bae]
= cheers

힘들다
[him-deul-da]
= to be tough, to be difficult, to be hard

취하다
[chwi-ha-da]
= to be drunk

택시
[taek-ssi]
= taxi, cab

아니요
[a-ni-yo]
= no

택시비
[taek-ssi-bi]
= taxi fare

지금
[ji-geum]
= now

타다
[ta-da]
= to ride

엄청
[eom-cheong]
= very, so

빨리
[ppal-li]
= quickly

감사하다
[gam-sa-ha-da]
= to be thankful

들어가다
[deu-reo-ga-da]
= to go in

왜
[wae]
= why

조금
[jo-geum]
= a little bit

마시다
[ma-si-da]
= to drink

많이
[ma-ni]
= many, much, a lot

취업하다
[chwi-eo-pa-da]
= to get a job

Grammar Points & Exercises

Study the two grammar points used in the dialogue and practice!

A. To Go Somewhere Using Transportation

(means of transportation) + 타고 가다
= to go by (means of transportation)

Track 149

Ex) 택시 + 타고 가다 → 택시 타고 가다 = to go by taxi

1. 버스 + 타고 가다 ……⟩ _____ = to go by bus

2. 지하철 + 타고 가다 ……⟩ _____ = to go by subway

B. Turning a Verb Into a Noun Phrase

VERB + -는 것 = VERB-ing, the act of VERB-ing

Ex) 취업하다 + -는 것* → 취업하는 것 = getting a job
* In daily conversation, people often pronounce 것 as 거.

3. 취하다 + -는 것 ……⟩ _____ = getting drunk

4. 들어가다 + -는 것 ……⟩ _____ = going in, the act of going in

Study the two pronunciation rules used in the dialogue and practice!

A. When a syllable ends with ㅂ and is followed by a syllable that begins with ㅎ, the ㅂ is combined with the ㅎ and is pronounced as ㅍ.

🔊) *Track 150*

    Ex) 취업하는 → [취어파는]

Write the pronunciations for the following words, just like the above example.

    1. 좁이다 (to narrow) ······> [   ]

    2. 급하게 (in a hurry) ······> [   ]

B. Take a moment to review some pronunciation rules that were previously covered.

    Ex) 삼겹살 → [삼겹쌀]

Write the pronunciations for the following phrases from the dialogue.

    3. 감사합니다 ······> [   ]

    4. 조금밖에 ······> [   ]

    5. 취했네 ······> [   ]

    6. 힘들었어요 ······> [   ]

Korean Only

Can you understand the entire dialogue without a translation? Test yourself!

- Short Dialogue

팀장: 선미 씨, 취했어?

선미: 아니요. 저 안 취했어요.

- Long Dialogue

선미: 팀장님! 건배!

팀장: 선미 씨, 취했어?

선미: 아니요! 저 안 취했어요.

팀장: 선미 씨 지금 엄청 취했어.

선미: 아니요. 저 안 취했어요. 팀장님, 감사합니다.

팀장: 왜?

선미: 저 조금밖에 안 마셨어요. 팀장님! 감사합니다!

팀장: 아이고, 많이 취했네.

선미: 감사합니다! 저 취업하는 거 힘들었어요. 감사합니다.

팀장: 자, 택시비. 택시 타고 빨리 들어가.

선미: 우와! 감사합니다, 팀장님. 감사합니다. 저 안 취했어요.

Answer Key for grammar exercises

1. 버스 타고 가다 *2.* 지하철 타고 가다 *3.* 취하는 것 *4.* 들어가는 것

Answer Key for pronunciation exercises

1. 조피다 *2.* 그파게 *3.* 감사함니다 *4.* 조금바께 *5.* 취핸네 *6.* 힘드러써요

Dialogue 26

질문 있어요.

I have a question.

•

Class

Short Dialogue with Translation

Start with a simple, two-line dialogue first!

 Track 151

성일: **선생님, 질문 있어요.**
Teacher, I have a question.

선생님: **질문하세요.**
Ask away.

Vocabulary

선생님 [seon-saeng-nim]	= *teacher*
질문 [jil-mun]	= *question*
있다 [it-tta]	= *to exist, to have*
질문하다 [jil-mu-na-da]	= *to ask*
-(으)세요 [-(eu)-se-yo]	= *imperative (polite)*

Cultural Tip

School calendars in Korea typically have summer vacation from mid-July until mid-August, and winter vacation from mid-December until the end of January. Students don't really have much of a break though, because they will continue to attend school during their vacation to prepare for the Korean college entrance exam, which is offered to third year high school students every November. Some students sign up for short courses or camps, while other students study by themselves at school in lieu of regular class. The entrance exam is so intense that even students in elementary school start studying during both summer and winter vacations to increase their chances of doing well!

Long Dialogue with Translation
Now challenge yourself with a longer dialogue!

○ 성일: **선생님, 질문 있어요.**
Teacher, I have a question.

◀)) *Track 153*

○ 선생님: **질문? 질문하세요.**
A question? Ask away.

○ 성일: **저희 방학 언제부터예요?**
When does our school vacation start?

○ 선생님: **방학? 방학은 7월부터예요.**
Vacation? The vacation starts in July.

○ 성일: **그럼 언제까지예요?**
Then, until when?

○ 선생님: **8월까지요.**
Until August.

○ 성일: **방학 때 저희 학교 나와요?**
Do we have to come to school during the vacation?

○ 선생님: **네. 고3은 학교 나와요.**
Yes. Senior students in high school have to come to school.

○ 성일: **그럼 도시락 싸 와요?**
Then, do we have to bring our lunch?

○ 선생님: **진석진! 다시 들어와요. 땡땡이는 안 돼요.**
Seokjin Jin, come back in. No cutting classes.

○ 성일: **선생님!**
Teacher!

○ 선생님: **이제 그만. 수업 시작할게요.**
Stop it now. I am going to start the class.

Vocabulary

선생님
[seon-saeng-nim]
= teacher

고3
[go-sam]
= senior student in high school, third year high school student

질문
[jil-mun]
= question

그럼
[geu-reom]
= then

있다
[it-tta]
= to exist, to have

도시락
[do-si-rak]
= lunch box

질문하다
[jil-mu-na-da]
= to ask

싸다
[ssa-da]
= to pack

저희
[jeo-hui]
= we, us (humble)

다시
[da-si]
= again

방학
[bang-hak]
= school vacation

들어오다
[deu-reo-o-da]
= to come in

언제
[eon-je]
= when

땡땡이
[ttaeng-ttaeng-i]
= cutting class

7월
[chi-rwol]
= July

이제
[i-je]
= now

8월
[pa-rwol]
= August

그만
[geu-man]
= stop

학교
[hak-kkyo]
= school

수업
[su-eop]
= class

나오다
[na-o-da]
= to come out

시작하다
[si-ja-ka-da]
= to start

Grammar Points & Exercises

Study the two grammar points used in the dialogue and practice!

A. Possession

NOUN + 있어요 = I have NOUN. / There is NOUN.

Ex) 질문 + 있어요 → 질문 있어요. = I have a question.

1. 도시락 + 있어요 ······⟩

_____ = I have a lunch box.
/ I brought my lunch.

2. 수업 + 있어요 ······⟩

_____ = I have a class.

B. Extended Time

NOUN + 부터 NOUN + 까지 = from NOUN to NOUN

Ex) 7월 + -부터 + 8월 + -까지 → 7월부터 8월까지 = from July to August

3. 월요일 + -부터 + 금요일 + -까지 ······⟩

_____ = from Monday
to Friday

4. 여기 + -부터 + 저기+ -까지 ······⟩

_____ = from here to there

Study the two pronunciation rules used in the dialogue and practice!

A. When a consonant is combined with ㅢ, the ㅢ is pronounced as ㅣ.

◀)) *Track 156*

Ex) 저희 → [저히]

Write the pronunciations for the following words, just like the above example.

1. 희망 (hope, wish) ······> [   ]

2. 무늬 (pattern) ······> [   ]

B. Time for a review!

Write the pronunciations for the following phrases from the dialogue.

3. 방학은 ······> [   ]

4. 학교 ······> [   ]

5. 들어와요 ······> [   ]

6. 시작할게요 ······> [   ]

Can you understand the entire dialogue without a translation? Test yourself!

- Short Dialogue

성일: 선생님, 질문 있어요.

선생님: 질문하세요.

- Long Dialogue

성일: 선생님, 질문 있어요.

선생님: 질문? 질문하세요.

성일: 저희 방학 언제부터예요?

선생님: 방학? 방학은 7월부터예요.

성일: 그럼 언제까지예요?

선생님: 8월까지요.

성일: 방학 때 저희 학교 나와요?

선생님: 네. 고3은 학교 나와요.

성일: 그럼 도시락 싸 와요?

선생님: 진석진! 다시 들어와요. 땡땡이는 안 돼요.

성일: 선생님!

선생님: 이제 그만. 수업 시작할게요.

Answer Key for grammar exercises

1. 도시락 있어요. *2*. 수업 있어요. *3*. 월요일부터 금요일까지 *4*. 여기부터 저기까지

Answer Key for pronunciation exercises

1. 히망 *2*. 무니 *3*. 방하근 *4*. 학꾜 *5*. 드러와요 *6*. 시자칼께요

시험 망쳤어.

I screwed up on my exam.

•

Exam

Short Dialogue with Translation
Start with a simple, two-line dialogue first!

현아: **야, 시험 잘 봤어?**
Hey, did you do well on your exam?

현석: **아니. 완전히 망쳤어.**
No, I completely screwed up.

Vocabulary

야
[ya]

= hey

시험 보다
[si-heom bo-da]

= to take a test

잘
[jal]

= well

아니.
[a-ni]

= No. (casual)

완전히
[wan-jeo-ni]

= completely

망치다
[mang-chi-da]

= to screw up

Cultural Tip

야 [ya] is the most informal way of addressing someone in Korean, and it is usually translated as "hey". It is extremely impolite to use when addressing someone older. Even adults who are the same age, unless they are very close with each other, do not use it. This word is commonly used between kids when addressing someone who is younger than themselves or who is of the same age.

Long Dialogue with Translation

Now challenge yourself with a longer dialogue!

현아: **야, 시험 잘 봤어?**
Hey, did you do well on your exam?

Track 159

현석: **아니. 완전히 망쳤어.**
No, I completely screwed up.

현아: **진짜? 다행이다.**
Really? That's a relief.

현석: **왜?**
Why?

현아: **나도 망쳤어.**
Because I screwed up, too.

현석: **진짜? 아휴. 나 이거 하나 틀렸어. 너 이거 맞았어?**
Really? (Sigh) I got the answer wrong for this one question.
Did you get this right?

현아: **뭐? 하나?**
What? One question?

현석: **응. 이거 하나 틀렸어. 그래서 백 점이 아니야.**
Yeah, I got this one question wrong. So I didn't get a full score.

현아: **너 맞고 싶어?**
Do you want to get beat up?

현석: **아니. 나 다음 달에는 백 점 맞을 거야. 나 간다.**
No. I will get a full score next month. I'm going now.

Vocabulary

시험 보다
[si-heom bo-da]
= to take a test

완전히
[wan-jeo-ni]
= completely

망치다
[mang-chi-da]
= to screw up

진짜
[jin-jja]
= really

다행
[da-haeng]
= relief

이거
[i-geo]
= this, this thing

하나
[ha-na]
= one

틀리다
[teul-li-da]
= to be wrong

맞다
[mat-tta]
= to be right

그래서
[geu-rae-seo]
= so

백 점
[baek jeom]
= perfect score, 100%

맞다
[mat-tta]
= to be beat up

다음
[da-eum]
= next

달
[dal]
= month

가다
[ga-da]
= to go

Grammar Points & Exercises

Study the two grammar points used in the dialogue and practice!

A. Conjunction: "so" or "therefore"

그래서 = therefore, so

* 그래서 is a conjunctive adverb, and is used at the beginning of the second phrase after the cause, grounds, or condition.

> **Ex)** 하나 틀렸어 + 그래서 + 백 점이 아니야 → 하나 틀렸어. 그래서 백 점이 아니야.
>
> = I got one wrong. So, I didn't get a full score.

1. 공부를 안 했어 + 그래서 + 시험을 망쳤어

······⟩ _____

= I didn't study. So, I screwed up on the exam.

2. 공부를 많이 했어 + 그래서 + 시험을 잘 봤어

······⟩ _____

= I studied a lot. Therefore, I did well on the exam.

B. Adverb: "also" or "too"

NOUN + -도 = NOUN also/too

> **Ex)** 나 + -도 → 나도 = I too

3. 이것 + -도 ······⟩ _____   = this one also

4. 다음 달 + -도 ……> _____ = next month too

Study the two pronunciation rules used in the dialogue and practice!

A. When a syllable ends with ㅈ and is followed by a syllable that begins with ㄱ, the ㄱ is pronounced as ㄲ.

) Track 162

Ex) 맞고 → [맏꼬]

* If you are wondering why 맞 is pronounced as 맏, please refer to page 66.

Write the pronunciations for the following words, just like the above example.

1. 갖고 ……> [   ]

2. 짖고 ……> [   ]

B. How well do you remember what's been covered already?

Write the pronunciations for the following phrases from the dialogue.

3. 완전히 ……> [   ]

4. 망쳤어 ……> [   ]

5. 백 점 ……> [   ]

6. 맞을 거야 ……> [   ]

Korean Only

Can you understand the entire dialogue without a translation? Test yourself!

- Short Dialogue

현아: 야, 시험 잘 봤어?

현석: 아니. 완전히 망쳤어.

- Long Dialogue

현아: 야, 시험 잘 봤어?

현석: 아니. 완전히 망쳤어.

현아: 진짜? 다행이다.

현석: 왜?

현아: 나도 망쳤어.

현석: 진짜? 아휴. 나 이거 하나 틀렸어. 너 이거 맞았어?

현아: 뭐? 하나?

현석: 응. 이거 하나 틀렸어. 그래서 백 점이 아니야.

현아: 너 맞고 싶어?

현석: 아니. 나 다음 달에는 백 점 맞을 거야. 나 간다.

Answer Key for grammar exercises

1. 공부를 안 했어. 그래서 시험을 망쳤어. *2.* 공부를 많이 했어. 그래서 시험을 잘 봤어.
3. 이것도 *4.* 다음 달도

Answer Key for pronunciation exercises

1. 갇꼬 *2.* 짇꼬 *3.* 완저니 *4.* 망쳐써 *5.* 백 쩜 *6.* 마즐 꺼야

여기 메뉴판이요.

Here is the menu.

•

Restaurant

Short Dialogue with Translation
Start with a simple, two-line dialogue first!

) *Track 163*

하림: **김치찌개 하나 주세요.**
Please give me one kimchi stew.

웨이터: **네. 알겠습니다.**
Ok. I got it.

Vocabulary

김치찌개 [gim-chi-jji-gae]	= *kimchi stew*
하나 [ha-na]	= *one*
주다 [ju-da]	= *to give*
-(으)세요 [-(eu)-se-yo]	= *imperative (polite)*
네. [ne.]	= *Yes. / Ok.*
알겠습니다. [al-get-sseum-ni-da]	= *I got it. / Yes, sir/ma'am. / I understand.*

Cultural Tip

In many Korean restaurants, there is a button on the table that you can push to ring a bell. This lets a server know that he/she is needed at your table. In loud or busy establishments, servers will often reply in unison with a simple word such as "네!" [ne!] to acknowledge that they have heard the call. If there is no button, or if you press the button but no one replies or comes to your table, you can get the attention of any server by saying "저기요!" [jeo-gi-yo!]

Long Dialogue with Translation

Now challenge yourself with a longer dialogue!

🔊 *Track 165*

하림: 저기요.
Excuse me.

웨이터: 네, 주문하세요.
Yes, please tell me your order.

하림: 김치찌개 하나 주세요.
Please give me one kimchi stew.

웨이터: 네. 알겠습니다.
Ok. I got it.

하림: 저기요. 김치찌개 매워요?
Excuse me. Is the kimchi stew spicy?

웨이터: 네. 저희 김치찌개는 많이 매워요.
Yes. Our kimchi stew is very spicy.

하림: 진짜요?
Really?

웨이터: 네. 된장찌개는 어때요? 된장찌개도 맛있어요.
Yes. How about soybean paste stew? Our soybean paste stew is good, too.

하림: 또 뭐 있어요?
What else do you have?

웨이터: 여기 메뉴판이요.
Here's the menu.

하림: 흠… 김치찌개 조금 덜 매운 거 없어요?
Hmm… Don't you have kimchi stew that's a little less spicy?

웨이터: 주방에 물어볼게요.
I'll ask the kitchen staff.

하림: 네. 감사합니다.
Ok. Thank you.

Vocabulary

주문하다 [ju-mu-na-da]	= to order	**또** [tto]	= again, else
김치찌개 [gim-chi-jji-gae]	= kimchi stew	**뭐** [mwo]	= what
하나 [ha-na]	= one	**메뉴판** [me-nyu-pan]	= menu
주다 [ju-da]	= to give	**조금** [jo-geum]	= a little
알다 [al-da]	= to know	**덜** [deol]	= less
저기요 [jeo-gi-yo]	= Excuse me.	**없다** [eop-tta]	= to not exist, to not have, to not be there
맵다 [maep-tta]	= to be spicy	**주방** [ju-bang]	= kitchen
많이 [ma-ni]	= many, much, a lot	**물어보다** [mu-reo-bo-da]	= to ask
진짜 [jin-jja]	= really	**감사하다** [gam-sa-ha-da]	= to be thankful
된장찌개 [doen-jang-jji-gae]	= soybean paste stew		
맛있다 [ma-sit-tta]	= to be tasty		

Grammar Points & Exercises

Study the two grammar points used in the dialogue and practice!

A. Less

덜 = less

Ex) 덜 + 맵다 → 덜 맵다 = to be less spicy

1. 덜 + 맛있다 ······> _____ = to be less tasty

2. 덜 + 감사하다 ······> _____ = to be less thankful

B. Introducing a New Relevant Subject

NOUN + -은/는 어때요? = How about NOUN?

* If the last syllable of the noun ends with a consonant, add -은 어때요. If the last syllable of the noun ends with a vowel, add -는 어때요.

Ex) 일 + -은/는 어때요? → 일은 어때요? = How about your work?

된장찌개 + -은/는 어때요? → 된장찌개는 어때요? = How about soybean paste stew?

3. 주방 + -은/는 어때요? ······> _____ = How about the kitchen?

4. 학교 + -은/는 어때요? ······> _____ = How about your school?

Study the two pronunciation rules used in the dialogue and practice!

A. When a syllable ends with ㅆ (which sounds the same as ㄷ when in the 받침 position) and is followed by a syllable that begins with ㅅ, the ㅅ is pronounced as ㅆ.

Ex) 알겠습니다 → [알겓씀니다]

* If you are wondering why 습니다 is pronounced 씀니다, not 씁니다, please refer to page 26.

Write the pronunciations for the following words, just like the above example.

1. 갔습니다 ·····> [   ]

2. 먹었습니다 ·····> [   ]

B. Let's review a few pronunciation rules that have been covered already.

Write the pronunciations for the following phrases from the dialogue.

3. 주문하세요 ·····> [   ]

4. 저희 ·····> [   ]

5. 많이 ·····> [   ]

6. 물어볼게요 ·····> [   ]

Korean Only

Can you understand the entire dialogue without a translation? Test yourself!

- Short Dialogue

하림: 김치찌개 하나 주세요.

웨이터: 네. 알겠습니다.

- Long Dialogue

하림: 저기요.

웨이터: 네, 주문하세요.

하림: 김치찌개 하나 주세요.

웨이터: 네. 알겠습니다.

하림: 저기요. 김치찌개 매워요?

웨이터: 네. 저희 김치찌개는 많이 매워요.

하림: 진짜요?

웨이터: 네. 된장찌개는 어때요? 된장찌개도 맛있어요.

하림: 또 뭐 있어요?

웨이터: 여기 메뉴판이요.

하림: 흠… 김치찌개 조금 덜 매운 거 없어요?

웨이터: 주방에 물어볼게요.

하림: 네. 감사합니다.

Answer Key for grammar exercises

1. 덜 맛있다 *2.* 덜 감사하다 *3.* 주방은 어때요? *4.* 학교는 어때요?

Answer Key for pronunciation exercises

1. 갇씀니다 *2.* 머걷씀니다* *3.* 주무나세요 *4.* 저히 *5.* 마니 *6.* 무러볼께요

* If you are wondering why 먹얻 is pronounced as 머걷, please refer to page 146.

Dialogue 29

아메리카노 한 잔 주세요.
Please give me one Americano.

•

Coffee Shop

Short Dialogue with Translation

Start with a simple, two-line dialogue first!

 Track 169

윤아: **아메리카노 한 잔 주세요.**
Give me one Americano, please.

직원: **네. 영수증 드릴까요?**
Ok. Would you like the receipt?

Vocabulary

아메리카노
[a-me-ri-ka-no]

= *Americano*

한 잔
[han jan]

= *one glass*

주다
[ju-da]

= *to give*

-(으)세요
[-(eu)-se-yo]

= *imperative (polite)*

네.
[ne.]

= *Yes. / Ok.*

영수증
[yeong-su-jeung]

= *receipt*

드리다
[deu-ri-da]

= *to give (honorific)*

VERB + -(으)ㄹ까요?
[-(eu)l-kka-yo?]

= *Shall we VERB?*

Cultural Tip

Korean coffee shops use Italian words for the names of coffee items, such as 카페 라
떼 [ka-pe la-tte] (caffé latte) or 카푸치노 [ka-pu-chi-no] (cappuccino). For other items besides
coffee, loanwords are usually used, which are just English words written in Hangeul
and pronounced with a Korean accent. Some common menu items that are loanwords
include 오렌지 주스 [o-ren-ji ju-sseu] (orange juice) and 캐모마일 티 [kae-mo-ma-il ti] (chamomile
tea).

Long Dialogue with Translation

Now challenge yourself with a longer dialogue!

Track 171

윤아: 아메리카노 한 잔 주세요.
Give me one Americano, please.

직원: 네. 영수증 드릴까요?
Ok. Would you like the receipt?

윤아: 아니요. 괜찮아요.
No. It's alright (to not receive it).

직원: 네. 진동벨 가져가세요.
Ok. Please take the pager.

윤아: 아, 죄송해요. 아이스로 바꿔 주세요.
Oh, I'm sorry. Please change it to iced.

직원: 아이스 아메리카노요?
Iced Americano?

윤아: 네.
Yes.

직원: 500원 더 비싸요. 그래서 취소하고 다시 결제해야 합니다.
It's 500 won more. So, you need to cancel the order and pay again.

윤아: 아, 진짜요? 흠…
Oh, really? Hmm…

직원: 아이스 아메리카노로 할까요?
Shall I make it an iced Americano?

윤아: 아니에요. 그냥 따뜻한 아메리카노 주세요.
No. Just give me a hot Americano.

직원: 네. 잠깐만 기다리세요.
Ok. Please wait just a moment.

Vocabulary

한 잔
[han jan]
= one glass

그래서
[geu-rae-seo]
= so

주다
[ju-da]
= to give

취소하다
[chwi-so-ha-da]
= to cancel

영수증
[yeong-su-jeung]
= receipt

다시
[da-si]
= again

드리다
[deu-ri-da]
= to glve (honorific)

결제하다
[gyeol-jje-ha-da]
= to pay

괜찮다
[gwaen-chan-ta]
= to be ok, to be alright

진짜
[jin-jja]
= really

진동벨
[jin-dong-bel]
= pager (call coaster)

하다
[ha-da]
= to do

가져가다
[ga-jyeo-ga-da]
= to take, to bring

그냥
[geu-nyang]
= just

죄송하다
[joe-song-ha-da]
= to be sorry

따뜻하다
[tta-tteu-ta-da]
= to be warm

아이스
[a-i-sseu]
= iced

잠깐만
[jam-kkan-man]
= just a moment

바꾸다
[ba-kku-da]
= to change

기다리다
[gi-da-ri-da]
= to wait

비싸다
[bi-ssa-da]
= to be expensive

Grammar Points & Exercises

Study the two grammar points used in the dialogue and practice!

A. Suggesting

NOUN + -(으)로 할까요? = Shall (I/we) go for NOUN?

Track 173

Ex) 아메리카노 + -(으)로 할까요? → 아메리카노로 할까요? = Shall (I/we) go for an Americano?

1. 김치찌개 + -(으)로 할까요?

⋯⋯〉 _____ = Shall (I/we) go for kimchi stew?

2. 오렌지 주스 + -(으)로 할까요?

⋯⋯〉 _____ = Shall (I/we) go for some orange juice?

B. Adjective: "more"

더 = more

Ex) 더 + 비싸다 → 더 비싸다 = to be more expensive

3. 더 + 기다리다 ⋯⋯〉 _____ = to wait more

4. 더 + 따뜻하다 ⋯⋯〉 _____ = to be warmer

Study the two pronunciation rules used in the dialogue and practice!

A. When a syllable ends with ㅅ (which sounds the same as ㄷ when in the 받침 position) and is followed by a syllable that begins with ㅎ, the ㅅ becomes part of the following syllable and is pronounced as ㅌ.

Ex) 따뜻한 → [따뜯한] → [따뜨탄]

Write the pronunciations for the following words, just like the above example.

1. 못하다 (to be bad at) ······> [   ]

2. 탓하다 (to blame) ······> [   ]

B. Take a moment to review some pronunciation rules that were previously covered.

Write the pronunciations for the following phrases from the dialogue.

3. 괜찮아요 ······> [   ]

4. 결제 ······> [   ]

5. 합니다 ······> [   ]

Korean Only

Can you understand the entire dialogue without a translation? Test yourself!

- Short Dialogue

윤아: 아메리카노 한 잔 주세요.

직원: 네. 영수증 드릴까요?

- Long Dialogue

윤아: 아메리카노 한 잔 주세요.

직원: 네. 영수증 드릴까요?

윤아: 아니요. 괜찮아요.

직원: 네. 진동벨 가져가세요.

윤아: 아, 죄송해요. 아이스로 바꿔 주세요.

직원: 아이스 아메리카노요?

윤아: 네.

직원: 500원 더 비싸요. 그래서 취소하고 다시 결제해야 합니다.

윤아: 아, 진짜요? 흠…

직원: 아이스 아메리카노로 할까요?

윤아: 아니에요. 그냥 따뜻한 아메리카노 주세요.

직원: 네. 잠깐만 기다리세요.

Answer Key for grammar exercises

1. 김치찌개로 할까요? *2.* 오렌지 주스로 할까요? *3.* 더 기다리다 *4.* 더 따뜻하다

Answer Key for pronunciation exercises

1. 모타다 *2.* 타타다 *3.* 괜차나요 *4.* 결쩨 *5.* 함니다

Dialogue 30

나 요리 잘해.

I am good at cooking.

•

Friend's House

Short Dialogue with Translation

Start with a simple, two-line dialogue first!

 Track 175

혜진: **이거 뭐야? 네가 다 만들었어?**
What is this? Did you make all of this?

현수: **응. 나 요리 잘해.**
Yeah. I'm good at cooking.

Vocabulary

이거 [i-geo]	= this, this thing	**응** [eung]	= yes, yeah, ok (casual)
NOUN + 뭐야? [mwo-ya?]	= What is NOUN? (casual)	**나** [na]	= I (casual)
다 [da]	= all	**요리** [yo-ri]	= cooking
만들다 [man-deul-da]	= to make	**잘하다** [ja-ra-da]	= to be good at, to do well

네
[ne]

= you (written)

* In colloquial Korean, it is often pronounced as 니 [ni] in order to avoid confusion with 내 [nae] meaning "I".

Cultural Tip

Toilet paper and laundry detergent are traditional Korean housewarming gifts. Some say that toilet paper represents a wish for the host family's problems to become untangled, similar to unrolling the tissue, while laundry detergent represents a wish for a prosperous life, as detergent makes more and more bubbles when used. Others say that toilet paper and laundry detergent wipe away bad luck because you clean with those items. On the other hand, toilet paper and laundry detergent are daily necessities, so the household will need them anyway. These days, since toilet paper and laundry detergent are cheap items, and most families have enough, people will give different items based on the host's tastes.

Long Dialogue with Translation

Now challenge yourself with a longer dialogue!

(Door bell rings and the door opens)

🔊 *Track 177*

현수: **들어와.**
Come on in.

혜진: **우와! 집 예쁘다!**
Wow. Your house is pretty!

현수: **그래? 고마워. 다른 애들은?**
Is it? Thank you. What about the others?

혜진: **금방 올 거야. 슈퍼 갔어.**
They will come here soon. They went to the store.

현수: **여기 앉아.**
Sit here.

혜진: **이거 뭐야? 네가 다 만들었어?**
What is this? Did you make all of this?

현수: **응. 나 요리 잘해.**
Yeah. I'm good at cooking.

혜진: **멋지다. 인테리어도 멋져. 그리고 음식도 맛있겠다.**
Cool. The interior design is cool, too. And the food seems delicious as well.

현수: **집들이 오늘이 처음이야.**
Today is my first time doing a housewarming party.

혜진: **진짜? 우리가 처음이야? 집 진짜 좋다.**
Really? Are we the first? Your house is really nice.

현수: **다행이다. 배고프지? 먼저 먹을래?**
Glad to hear that. You must be hungry. Do you want to eat first?

혜진: **아니. 기다릴게. 애들 왜 안 오지?**
No, I'll wait. Why aren't they coming?

Vocabulary

들어오다 [deu-reo-o-da]	= to come in		요리 [yo-ri]	= cooking
집 [jip]	= house, home		잘하다 [ja-ra-da]	= to be good at, to do well
예쁘다 [ye-ppeu-da]	= to be pretty		멋지다 [meot-jji-da]	= to be cool
고맙다 [go-map-tta]	= to be thankful		인테리어 [in-te-ri-eo]	= interior design
다른 [da-reun]	= different		음식 [eum-sik]	= food
애들 [ae-deul]	= other (friends)		맛있다 [ma-sit-tta]	= to be tasty
금방 [geum-bang]	= soon		집들이 [jip-tteu-ri]	= housewarming party
오다 [o-da]	= to come		오늘 [o-neul]	= today
슈퍼 [syu-peo]	= grocery store, supermarket		처음 [cheo-eum]	= first
가다 [ga-da]	= to go		다행 [da-haeng]	= relief
여기 [yeo-gi]	= here		배고프다 [bae-go-peu-da]	= to be hungry
앉다 [an-tta]	= to sit		먼저 [meon-jeo]	= first, early
뭐 [mwo]	= what		기다리다 [gi-da-ri-da]	= to wait
다 [da]	= all			

Grammar Points & Exercises

Study the two grammar points used in the dialogue and practice!

A. Capable at Something

NOUN + 잘해(요) = (SUBJECT) am/is/are good at NOUN

Ex) 요리 + 잘해(요) → 요리 잘해(요). = (They) are good at cooking.

1. 수영 + 잘해(요) ······〉 _____ = (They) are good at swimming.

2. 축구 + 잘해(요) ······〉 _____ = (They) are good at soccer.

B. Exclamation - Seeking Agreement

-지(요)? = (SUBJECT) (VERB/ADJECTIVE), right?

Ex) 배고프다 + -지(요)? → 배고프지(요)? = You are hungry, right?

3. 잘하다 + -지(요)? ······〉 _____ = (They) are good at it, right?

4. 예쁘다 + -지(요)? ······〉 _____ = (It) is pretty, right?

Study the two pronunciation rules used in the dialogue and practice!

A. When a word or syllable ends with ㄵ and is not followed by anything or is followed by a consonant, ㄵ is pronounced as ㄴ.

Ex) 앉 → [안]

B. When ㄵ is followed by a syllable that begins with a vowel, the ㅈ becomes part of the following syllable.

Ex) 앉아 → [안자]

Write the pronunciations for the following words, just like the above example.

1. 앉았어요 ······> [   ]

2. 앉아서 ······> [   ]

Korean Only

Can you understand the entire dialogue without a translation? Test yourself!

- Short Dialogue

혜진: 이거 뭐야? 네가 다 만들었어?

현수: 응. 나 요리 잘해.

- Long Dialogue

현수: 들어와.

혜진: 우와! 집 예쁘다!

현수: 그래? 고마워. 다른 애들은?

혜진: 금방 올 거야. 슈퍼 갔어.

현수: 여기 앉아.

혜진: 이거 뭐야? 네가 다 만들었어?

현수: 응. 나 요리 잘해.

혜진: 멋지다. 인테리어도 멋져. 그리고 음식도 맛있겠다.

현수: 집들이 오늘이 처음이야.

혜진: 진짜? 우리가 처음이야? 집 진짜 좋다.

현수: 다행이다. 배고프지? 먼저 먹을래?

혜진: 아니. 기다릴게. 애들 왜 안 오지?

Answer Key for grammar exercises

1. 수영 잘해(요). *2.* 축구 잘해(요). *3.* 잘하지(요)? *4.* 예쁘지(요)?

Answer Key for pronunciation exercises

1. 안자써요* *2.* 안자서

* If you are wondering why 안잤어요 *is pronounced as* 안자써요, *please refer to page 162.*

이제 물 부어.

Now pour in some water.

•

Cooking

Track 181

Short Dialogue with Translation

Start with a simple, two-line dialogue first!

상미: **참치 캔 따 줘**.
Open the tuna can for me.

승우: **응. 여기**.
Ok. Here.

Vocabulary

참치 [cham-chi]	= *tuna*
캔 [kaen]	= *can*
따다 [tta-da]	= *to open*
VERB + **-아/어/여 줘** [-a/eo/yeo jwo]	= *Please VERB (me). (casual)*
응 [eung]	= *yes, yeah, ok (casual)*
여기 [yeo-gi]	= *here*

Cultural Tip

Cooking-related TV shows have recently become very popular in Korea. There are also many chefs who have become famous, too. In addition to chefs, some restaurant owners who happen to cook well are also popular on TV, since they usually introduce simple, yet delicious recipes of their own that are easy to cook at home. The rise in popularity of cooking shows has led many young people to dream of becoming a chef.

Long Dialogue with Translation

Now challenge yourself with a longer dialogue!

상미: **오늘 저녁은 참치 김치찌개야.**
Today we are having tuna kimchi stew for dinner.

Track 183

승우: **우와! 맛있겠다!**
Wow. It sounds delicious!

상미: **오늘은 네가 도와줘.**
You need to help me today.

승우: **내가? 나 요리 못해.**
Me? I can't cook.

상미: **참치 김치찌개는 진짜 쉬워. 네가 할래?**
Tuna kimchi stew is really easy. Do you want to make it?

승우: **도와줄게.**
I'll help you.

상미: **먼저 참치 캔 따 줘.**
First, open the tuna can.

승우: **응. 여기.**
Ok. Here.

상미: **참치 기름에 김치를 볶아.**
Stir-fry the kimchi in the tuna oil.

승우: **나 김치 볶음도 좋아해. 그냥 이거 먹자.**
I like fried kimchi, too. Let's just eat this.

상미: **기다려. 금방 해. 이제 물 부어.**
Wait. We can do it soon. Now, pour in some water.

승우: **응. 그리고 뭐 해?**
Ok. And now what?

상미: **참치 넣어. 끝.**
Add tuna. The end.

Vocabulary

오늘
[o-neul]
= today

김치 볶음
[gim-chi bo-kkeum]
= fried kimchi

저녁
[jeo-nyeok]
= dinner, evening

좋아하다
[jo-a-ha-da]
= to like

김치찌개
[gim-chi-jji-gae]
= kimchi stew

그냥
[geu-nyang]
= just

맛있다
[ma-sit-tta]
= to be tasty

이거
[i-geo]
= this, this thing

도와주다
[do-wa-ju-da]
= to help

먹다
[meok-tta]
= to eat

요리
[yo-ri]
= cooking

기다리다
[gi-da-ri-da]
= to wait

못하다
[mo-ta-da]
= to be bad at

금방
[geum-bang]
= soon

진짜
[jin-jja]
= really

물
[mul]
= water

쉽다
[swip-tta]
= to be easy

붓다
[but-tta]
= to pour

먼저
[meon-jeo]
= first, early

그리고
[geu-ri-go]
= and

기름
[gi-reum]
= oil

넣다
[neo-ta]
= to put, to add

볶다
[bok-tta]
= to fry

끝
[kkeut]
= end

네
[ne]
= you (written)

* In colloquial Korean, it is often pronounced as 니 [ni] in order to avoid confusion with 내 [nae] meaning "I".

Grammar Points & Exercises
Study the two grammar points used in the dialogue and practice!

A. Asking Politely

Track 185

VERB + -아/어/여 줘 = Please VERB (for me). (casual)

Ex) 따다 + -아/어/여 줘 → 따아 줘 → 따 줘. = Please open it (for me).

1. 볶다 + 아/어/여 줘 ……⟩ _____ = Please fry it (for me).

2. 기다리다 + 아/어/여 줘 ……⟩ _____ = Please wait (for me).

B. Asking for an Opinion/Seeking a Response

ADJECTIVE + -(으)ㄹ까(요)? = Do you think (SUBJECT) will be ADJECTIVE? / I wonder if (SUBJECT) will be ADJECTIVE.

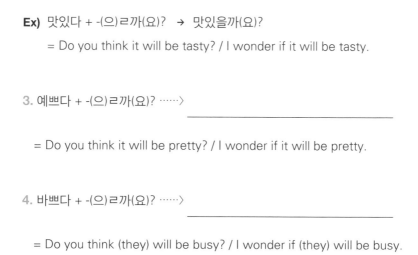

Ex) 맛있다 + -(으)ㄹ까(요)? → 맛있을까(요)?

= Do you think it will be tasty? / I wonder if it will be tasty.

3. 예쁘다 + -(으)ㄹ까(요)? ……⟩ _____

= Do you think it will be pretty? / I wonder if it will be pretty.

4. 바쁘다 + -(으)ㄹ까(요)? ……⟩ _____

= Do you think (they) will be busy? / I wonder if (they) will be busy.

Study the two pronunciation rules used in the dialogue and practice!

A. When ㅌ is used as 받침, or a final consonant, it is pronounced like ㄷ.

◀)) *Track 186*

Ex) 끝 → [끋]

Write the pronunciations for the following words, just like the above example.

1. 밭 (dry field, farm) ……⟩ [   ]

2. 뭍 (land, shore) ……⟩ [   ]

B. When a syllable ends with ㅆ (which sounds the same as ㄷ when in the 받침 position) and is followed by a syllable that begins with ㄱ, the ㄱ is pronounced as ㄲ.

Ex) 맛있겠 → [마싣껟]

Write the pronunciations for the following words, just like the above example.

3. 있고 ……⟩ [   ]

4. 봤고 ……⟩ [   ]

Korean Only

Can you understand the entire dialogue without a translation? Test yourself!

- Short Dialogue

상미: 참치 캔 따 줘.

승우: 응. 여기.

- Long Dialogue

상미: 오늘 저녁은 참치 김치찌개야.

승우: 우와! 맛있겠다!

상미: 오늘은 네가 도와줘.

승우: 내가? 나 요리 못해.

상미: 참치 김치찌개는 진짜 쉬워. 네가 할래?

승우: 도와줄게.

상미: 먼저 참치 캔 따 줘.

승우: 응. 여기.

상미: 참치 기름에 김치를 볶아.

승우: 나 김치 볶음도 좋아해. 그냥 이거 먹자.

상미: 기다려. 금방 해. 이제 물 부어.

승우: 응. 그리고 뭐 해?

상미: 참치 넣어. 끝.

Answer Key for grammar exercises

1. 볶아 줘. *2.* 기다려 줘. *3.* 예쁠까(요)? *4.* 바쁠까(요)?

Answer Key for pronunciation exercises

1. 받 *2.* 묻 *3.* 읽꼬 *4.* 밭꼬

지금 배달 돼요?

Can you deliver now?

•

Ordering Delivery

Short Dialogue with Translation

Start with a simple, two-line dialogue first!

성원: **지금 배달 돼요?**
Can you deliver now?

직원: **네. 주소 말해 주세요.**
Yes. Please tell me your address.

Vocabulary

지금
[ji-geum]

= now

배달
[bae-dal]

= delivery

되다
[doe-da]

= to work, to be available

네.
[ne.]

= Yes. / Ok.

주소
[ju-so]

= address

말해 주다
[ma-rae ju-da]

= to tell

Cultural Tip

People in Korea order food for delivery over the phone quite frequently because it is incredibly convenient. Fried chicken is the most popular delivery food, but the word for "fried chicken" in Korean is just 치킨 [chi-kin], which is the English loanword "chicken" but written in Hangeul and pronounced with a Korean accent. The native Korean word 닭 [dak] is used to refer to chicken which is not fried.

Long Dialogue with Translation

Now challenge yourself with a longer dialogue!

Track 189

직원: **한국 치킨입니다.**
This is Hanguk Chicken.

성원: **지금 배달 돼요?**
Can you deliver now?

직원: **네. 주소 말해 주세요.**
Yes. Please tell me your address.

성원: **서울시 마포구 망원동이요.**
It's Mang-won dong, Mapo-Gu, Seoul.

직원: **어떤 치킨 드릴까요?**
What kind of chicken would you like?

성원: **후라이드 반, 양념 반이요. 얼마예요?**
Half fried, half marinated. How much is it?

직원: 15,000**원이요.**
It's 15,000 won.

성원: **맥주도 주세요.**
Beer, too.

직원: 18,000**원입니다.**
It's 18,000 won.

성원: **얼마나 걸려요?**
How long will it take?

직원: 30**분이요.**
30 minutes.

성원: **네. 카드로 결제할게요.**
Yes. I will pay with a credit card.

직원: **네, 알겠습니다.**
Ok. I got it.

Vocabulary

한국 [han-guk]	= Korea
지금 [ji-geum]	= now
배달 [bae-dal]	= delivery
되다 [doe-da]	= to work, to be available
주소 [ju-so]	= address
말해 주다 [ma-rae ju-da]	= to tell
어떤 [eo-tteon]	= which, what kind of
드리다 [deu-ri-da]	= to give (honorific)
반 [ban]	= half
얼마 [eol-ma]	= how much
맥주 [maek-jju]	= beer
주다 [ju-da]	= to give
얼마나 [eol-ma-na]	= how
걸리다 [geol-li-da]	= to take (time)
카드 [ka-deu]	= credit card
결제하다 [gyeol-jje-ha-da]	= to pay

Grammar Points & Exercises

Study the two grammar points used in the dialogue and practice!

A. Asking Politely for an Additional Item

NOUN + -도 주세요 = Please give me NOUN, too.

Ex) 맥주 + -도 주세요 → 맥주도 주세요. = Please give me beer, too.

1. 카드 + -도 주세요 ······⟩

_____ = Please give me a card, too.

2. 주소 + -도 주세요 ······⟩

_____ = Please give me your address, too.

B. Asking Availability

NOUN + 돼요? = Is NOUN available? / Do you VERB?

Ex) 배달 + 돼요? → 배달 돼요? = Is delivery available? / Do you deliver?

3. 치킨 + 돼요? ······⟩

_____

= Is fried chicken available? / Do you serve fried chicken?

4. 카드 + 돼요? ······⟩

_____

= Is (credit) card available? / Do you accept (credit) cards?

Study the two pronunciation rules used in the dialogue and practice!

A. When a syllable ends with ㅂ and is followed by a syllable that begins with ㅂ, the second ㅂ is pronounced as ㅃ.

Ex) 삼십 분 (30 minutes) → [삼십 뿐]

Write the pronunciations for the following words, just like the above example.

1. 육십 분 (60 minutes) ······> [   ]

2. 답변 (answer, reply) ······> [   ]

B. Time for a review!

Write the pronunciations for the following phrases from the dialogue.

3. 치킨입니다 ······> [   ]

4. 말해 ······> [   ]

5. 맥주도 ······> [   ]

6. 결제할게요 ······> [   ]

Korean Only

Can you understand the entire dialogue without a translation? Test yourself!

- Short Dialogue

성원: 지금 배달 돼요?

직원: 네. 주소 말해 주세요.

- Long Dialogue

직원: 한국 치킨입니다.

성원: 지금 배달 돼요?

직원: 네. 주소 말해 주세요.

성원: 서울시 마포구 망원동이요.

직원: 어떤 치킨 드릴까요?

성원: 후라이드 반, 양념 반이요. 얼마예요?

직원: 15,000원이요.

성원: 맥주도 주세요.

직원: 18,000원입니다.

성원: 얼마나 걸려요?

직원: 30분이요.

성원: 네. 카드로 결제할게요.

직원: 네, 알겠습니다.

Answer Key for grammar exercises

1. 카드도 주세요. *2.* 주소도 주세요. *3.* 치킨 돼요? *4.* 카드 돼요?

Answer Key for pronunciation exercises

1. 육씹 뿐* *2.* 답뻔 *3.* 치키님니다 *4.* 마래 *5.* 맥쭈도 *6.* 결쩨할께요

* *If you are wondering why* 육십 *is pronounced as* 육씹, *please refer to page 202.*

감기약 주세요.

Please give me some cold medicine.

•

Pharmacy

Short Dialogue with Translation
Start with a simple, two-line dialogue first!

Track 193

약사: **어디가 아프세요?**
What's bothering you?

수정: **목이 아파요.**
My throat hurts.

Vocabulary

어디 [eo-di]	= where
아프다 [a-peu-da]	= to be sick, to hurt
VERB/ADJECTIVE + -세요? [-se-yo?]	= Do you VERB? / Are you ADJECTIVE? (honorific)
목 [mok]	= throat

Cultural Tip

When you visit a pharmacy in Korea to have a prescription filled, you may receive small packets of medicine that are already separated into individual doses. However, there are usually no instructions on the packets, so you will have to speak with the pharmacist who will be more familiar with the doctor's prescription. People in Korea tend to visit the pharmacy closest to the doctor's office or hospital to fill their prescription. If you need an English-speaking pharmacist, then you can go to that pharmacy to have it filled.

Long Dialogue with Translation

Now challenge yourself with a longer dialogue!

수정: **감기약 주세요.**
Please give me some cold medicine.

약사: **어디가 아프세요?**
What's bothering you?

수정: **목이 아파요.**
My throat hurts.

약사: **기침도 하세요?**
Do you have a cough, too?

수정: **기침은 안 해요.**
I don't have a cough.

약사: **콧물은요?**
Do you have a runny nose?

수정: **콧물 안 나요.**
I don't have a runny nose.

약사: **두통은 있어요?**
Do you have a headache?

수정: **아니요. 그런데 열이 있어요.**
No. But I have a fever.

약사: **지금 열나세요?**
Do you have a fever now?

수정: **네.**
Yes.

약사: **이거랑 이거 하루에 세 번 드세요.**
Take this and this three times a day.

수정: **한 알씩이요?**
One pill each?

약사: **이거는 두 알씩 드세요.**
This one, two pills each time.

수정: **얼마예요?**
How much is it?

약사: **5,000원이에요.**
5,000 won.

수정: **여기요. 감사합니다.**
Here. Thank you.

Vocabulary

감기약
[gam-gi-yak]
= cold medicine

열
[yeol]
= fever

주다
[ju-da]
= to give

열나다
[yeol-la-da]
= to have a fever

어디
[eo-di]
= where

이거
[i-geo]
= this, this thing

아프다
[a-peu-da]
= to be sick, to hurt

하루
[ha-ru]
= one day

목
[mok]
= throat

세 번
[se beon]
= three times

기침
[gi-chim]
= cough

드시다
[deu-si-da]
= to eat (honorific)

하다
[ha-da]
= to do

한 알
[han al]
= one pill

콧물
[kon-mul]
= snot

씩
[ssik]
= each

콧물 나다
[kon-mul na-da]
= to have a runny nose

얼마
[eol-ma]
= how much

두통
[du-tong]
= headache

여기
[yeo-gi]
= here

있다
[it-tta]
= to exist, to have

그런데
[geu-reon-de]
= but, however

Grammar Points & Exercises

Study the two grammar points used in the dialogue and practice!

A. Negative Statement

안 + VERB/ADJECTIVE + -아/어/여요
= I do not VERB. / I am not ADJECTIVE.

Ex) 안 + 하다 + -아/어/여요 → 안 해요. = I don't do (it).

1. 안 + 아프다 + -아/어/여요 ⋯⋯〉 _____ = I am not sick.

2. 안 + 주다 + -아/어/여요 ⋯⋯〉 _____ = I do not give (it).

B. Definitive Frequency

PERIOD OF TIME + -에 + NUMERAL DETERMINER + 번
= NUMBER time(s) a PERIOD OF TIME

Ex) 일 년 + -에 + 한 + 번 → 일 년에 한 번 = once a year

3. 하루 + -에 + 한 + 번 ⋯⋯〉 _____ = once a day

4. 한 달 + -에 + 두 + 번 ⋯⋯〉 _____ = twice a month

Study the two pronunciation rules used in the dialogue and practice!

A. When a syllable ends with ㅅ (which sounds the same as ㄷ when in the 받침 position) and is followed by a syllable that begins with ㅁ, the ㅅ is pronounced as ㄴ.

◀)) *Track 198*

Ex) 콧물 → [콛물] → [콘물]

Write the pronunciations for the following words, just like the above example.

1. 툇마루 ·····> [   ]

2. 뱃머리 ·····> [   ]

B. When a syllable ends with ㄹ and is followed by a syllable that begins with ㄴ, the ㄴ is pronounced as ㄹ.

Ex) 열나세요 → [열라세요]

Write the pronunciations for the following words, just like the above example.

3. 불나요 ·····> [   ]

4. 찰나 ·····> [   ]

Korean Only

Can you understand the entire dialogue without a translation? Test yourself!

- Short Dialogue

약사: 어디가 아프세요?

수정: 목이 아파요.

- Long Dialogue

수정: 감기약 주세요.

약사: 어디가 아프세요?

수정: 목이 아파요.

약사: 기침도 하세요?

수정: 기침은 안 해요.

약사: 콧물은요?

수정: 콧물 안 나요.

약사: 두통은 있어요?

수정: 아니요. 그런데 열이 있어요.

약사: 지금 열나세요?

수정: 네.

약사: 이거랑 이거 하루에 세 번 드세요.

수정: 한 알씩이요?

약사: 이거는 두 알씩 드세요.

수정: 얼마예요?

약사: 5,000원이에요.

수정: 여기요. 감사합니다.

Answer Key for grammar exercises

1. 안 아파요. *2.* 안 줘요. *3.* 하루에 한 번 *4.* 한 달에 두 번

Answer Key for pronunciation exercises

1. 퇸마루 *2.* 밴머리 *3.* 불라요 *4.* 찰라

배가 아파요.

My stomach hurts.

•

Hospital

Short Dialogue with Translation
Start with a simple, two-line dialogue first!

◀⦿) *Track 199*

수진: **배가 아파요.**
My stomach hurts.

의사: **설사하셨어요?**
Did you have diarrhea?

Vocabulary

배
[bae]

= stomach

아프다
[a-peu-da]

= to be sick, to hurt

설사하다
[seol-ssa-ha-da]

= to have diarrhea

VERB + -셨어요?
[-syeo-sseo-yo?]

= Did you VERB? (honorific)

Cultural Tip

According to statistical data from the Korean Health Insurance Review & Assessment Service, the most common reason why people in Korea visit the doctor's office is for acute bronchitis. When it comes to more serious conditions which require hospitalization, the top two most common reasons are gastroenteritis and disk problems in the neck or back. Due to the use of computers and smartphones, the number of people who are suffering from forward head posture is increasing dramatically.

Long Dialogue with Translation

Now challenge yourself with a longer dialogue!

수진: 배가 아파요.
My stomach hurts.

Track 201

의사: **설사하셨어요?**
Did you have diarrhea?

수진: **네. 어제 설사했어요.**
Yes, I had diarrhea yesterday.

의사: **오늘도 설사하셨어요?**
Did you have diarrhea today, too?

수진: **아니요. 오늘은 안 했어요.**
No, not today.

의사: **열이 있으세요.**
You have a fever.

수진: **진짜요?**
Really?

의사: **네. 39도예요.**
Yes. It's 39 degrees [Celsius].

수진: **아…**
Oh...

의사: **장염이에요.**
It's enteritis.

수진: **장염이요?**
Enteritis?

의사: **네. 따뜻한 물 많이 드세요. 고기랑 술 드시지 마세요.**
Yes. Drink a lot of hot water. Don't eat meat or drink alcohol.

수진: **아… 네… 감사합니다.**
Oh...I see...Thank you.

Vocabulary

배
[bae]
= stomach

아프다
[a-peu-da]
= to be sick, to hurt

설사하다
[seol-ssa-ha-da]
= to have diarrhea

어제
[eo-je]
= yesterday

오늘
[o-neul]
= today

열
[yeol]
= fever

진짜
[jin-jja]
= really

장염
[jang-yeom]
= enteritis

따뜻하다
[tta-tteu-ta-da]
= to be warm

물
[mul]
= water

많이
[ma-ni]
= many, much, a lot

드시다
[deu-si-da]
= to eat (honorific)

고기
[go-gi]
= meat

술
[sul]
= alcoholic drink

감사하다
[gam-sa-ha-da]
= to be thankful

Grammar Points & Exercises

Study the two grammar points used in the dialogue and practice!

A. Making an Inquiry

VERB + -시- + -았/었/였어요? = Did you VERB? (honorific)

Ex) 설사하다 + -시- + -았/었/였어요? → 설사하셨어요? = Did you have diarrhea?

1. 식사하다 + -시- + -았/었/였어요?

⋯⋯⟩ _____ = Did you eat? / Have you eaten?

2. 공부하다 + -시- + -았/었/였어요?

⋯⋯⟩ _____ = Did you study?

B. Negative Imperative

VERB + -지 마세요 = Don't VERB. (honorific)

Ex) 드시다 + -지 마세요 → 드시지 마세요. = Don't eat.

3. 하다 + -지 마세요 ⋯⋯⟩ _____ = Don't do (it). / Stop (it).

4. 오다 + -지 마세요 ⋯⋯⟩ _____ = Don't come.

Study the two pronunciation rules used in the dialogue and practice!

A. For Sino-Korean words (words influenced by hanja or Chinese characters), when a syllable ends with ㄹ and is followed by a syllable that begins with ㅅ, the ㅅ is pronounced as ㅆ.

Ex) 설사 → [설싸]

Write the pronunciations for the following words, just like the above example.

1. 일시 ·····> [   ]

2. 말살 ·····> [   ]

B. Let's review a few pronunciation rules that have been covered already.

Write the pronunciations for the following phrases from the dialogue.

3. 장염이에요 ·····> [   ]

4. 따뜻한 ·····> [   ]

5. 많이 ·····> [   ]

6. 감사합니다 ·····> [   ]

Korean Only

Can you understand the entire dialogue without a translation? Test yourself!

- Short Dialogue

수진: 배가 아파요.

의사: 설사하셨어요?

- Long Dialogue

수진: 배가 아파요.

의사: 설사하셨어요?

수진: 네. 어제 설사했어요.

의사: 오늘도 설사하셨어요?

수진: 아니요. 오늘은 안 했어요.

의사: 열이 있으세요.

수진: 진짜요?

의사: 네. 39도예요.

수진: 아…

의사: 장염이에요.

수진: 장염이요?

의사: 네. 따뜻한 물 많이 드세요. 고기랑 술 드시지 마세요.

수진: 아… 네… 감사합니다.

Answer Key for grammar exercises

1. 식사하셨어요? *2*. 공부하셨어요? *3*. 하지 마세요. *4*. 오지 마세요.

Answer Key for pronunciation exercises

1. 일씨 *2*. 말쌀 *3*. 장여미에요 *4*. 따뜨탄 *5*. 마니 *6*. 감사함니다

Dialogue 35

요즘 매일 피곤해.
These days, I feel tired every day.

•

Not Feeling Well

Short Dialogue with Translation
Start with a simple, two-line dialogue first!

Track 205

형식: **무슨 일 있어?**
What's wrong?

수희: **아니. 요즘 매일 피곤해.**
Nothing. These days, I feel tired every day.

Vocabulary

무슨
[mu-seun]
= what

일
[il]
= work, happening

있다
[it-tta]
= to exist, to have

아니.
[a-ni.]
= No. (casual)

요즘
[yo-jeum]
= these days

매일
[mae-il]
= everyday

피곤하다
[pi-go-na-da]
= to be tired

Cultural Tip

You may be surprised at how often people in Korea visit the doctor's office. Since many people see the doctor even if they have a minor cold, you may be told that you should go to the doctor's office when you look pale or sick, even if just a little. The doctor's office and the hospital are both called 병원 [byeong-won] in Korean; therefore, if someone tells you that you should go to the 병원, be sure to find out if that person meant the hospital or the doctor's office.

Long Dialogue with Translation
Now challenge yourself with a longer dialogue!

Track 207

수희: 아, 피곤해.
Ah, I'm tired.

형식: 무슨 일 있어?
What's wrong?

수희: 아니. 요즘 매일 피곤해.
Nothing. These days, I feel tired every day.

형식: 그래? 어디 아파? 감기?
Really? Are you sick? A cold?

수희: 감기 아니야. 그냥 졸려. 그리고 소화가 안 돼.
It's not a cold. I'm just sleepy. And I have indigestion.

형식: 진짜? 왜 소화가 안 돼?
Really? Why do you have indigestion?

수희: 몰라. 이상해.
I don't know. It's strange.

형식: 병원에 가 봐.
Go to the hospital.

수희: 병원?
The hospital?

형식: 응. 언제부터 그랬어?
Yeah. Since when did you feel like this?

수희: 한 달 정도 됐어.
It's been about a month.

형식: 한 달? 야, 빨리 병원 가.
A month? Hurry up and go to the hospital.

Vocabulary

피곤하다
[pi-go-na-da]
= to be tired

되다
[doe-da]
= to work, to be done

무슨
[mu-seun]
= what

진짜
[jin-jja]
= really

일
[il]
= work, happening

왜
[wae]
= why

요즘
[yo-jeum]
= these days

모르다
[mo-reu-da]
= to now know

매일
[mae-il]
= everyday

이상하다
[i-sang-ha-da]
= to be strange

어디
[eo-di]
= where

병원
[byeong-won]
= hospital, doctor's office

아프다
[a-peu-da]
= to be sick, to hurt

가다
[ga-da]
= to go

감기
[gam-gi]
= cold

언제
[eon-je]
= when

그냥
[geu-nyang]
= just

한 달
[han dal]
= one month

졸리다
[jol-li-da]
= to be sleepy

정도
[jeong-do]
= about, around

소화
[so-hwa]
= digestion

빨리
[ppal-li]
= quickly

Grammar Points & Exercises

Study the two grammar points used in the dialogue and practice!

A. Negative

NOUN + 아니야 = It's not NOUN. (casual)

> **Ex)** 감기 + 아니야 → 감기 아니야. = It's not a cold.

1. 책 + 아니야 ······⟩ _____ = It's not a book.

2. 병원 + 아니야 ······⟩ _____ = It's not a hospital.

B. Approximate Frequency

PERIOD OF TIME + 정도 됐어(요) = It has been about PERIOD OF TIME.

> **Ex)** 한 달 + 정도 됐어(요) → 한 달 정도 됐어(요).
> = It has been about a month.

3. 일주일 + 정도 됐어(요) ······⟩ _____ = It has been about a week.

4. 일 년 + 정도 됐어(요) ······⟩ _____ = It has been about a year.

Study the two pronunciation rules used in the dialogue and practice!

A. When there are two separate words, if the first word ends with ㄴ and the second word begins with 이, a ㄴ is added so 이 is pronounced as 니.

◀) **Track 210**

Ex) 무슨 일 → [무슨 닐] (O)

무슨 일 → [무스 닐] (X)

Write the pronunciations for the following words, just like the above example

1. 바쁜 일 ……> [   ]

2. 좋은 일 ……> [   ]

B. How well do you remember what's been covered already?

Write the pronunciations for the following phrases from the dialogue.

3. 피곤해 ……> [   ]

4. 병원에 ……> [   ]

5. 그랬어 ……> [   ]

6. 됐어 ……> [   ]

Korean Only

Can you understand the entire dialogue without a translation? Test yourself!

- Short Dialogue

형식: 무슨 일 있어?

수희: 아니. 요즘 매일 피곤해.

- Long Dialogue

수희: 아, 피곤해.

형식: 무슨 일 있어?

수희: 아니. 요즘 매일 피곤해.

형식: 그래? 어디 아파? 감기?

수희: 감기 아니야. 그냥 졸려. 그리고 소화가 안 돼.

형식: 진짜? 왜 소화가 안 돼?

수희: 몰라. 이상해.

형식: 병원에 가 봐.

수희: 병원?

형식: 응. 언제부터 그랬어?

수희: 한 달 정도 됐어.

형식: 한 달? 야, 빨리 병원 가.

Answer Key for grammar exercises

1. 책 아니야. 2. 병원 아니야. 3. 일주일 정도 됐어(요). 4. 일 년 정도 됐어(요).

Answer Key for pronunciation exercises

1. 바쁜 닐 2. 조은 닐* 3. 피고내 4. 병워네 5. 그래써 6. 돼써

* If you are wondering why 좋은 is pronounced as 조은, please refer to page 154.

Dialogue 36

교통 카드로 할게요.
I will pay with a transportation card.

•

Taxi

Short Dialogue with Translation

Start with a simple, two-line dialogue first!

 Track 211

택시 기사: **다 왔습니다.**
We are here.

수정: **교통 카드로 할게요.**
I will pay with a transportation card.

Vocabulary

다 [da]	= all	카드 [ka-deu]	= card
오다 [o-da]	= to come	-(으)로 [-(eu)-ro]	= with
교통 [gyo-tong]	= transportation, traffic	하다 [ha-da]	= to do
VERB ㅣ 았/었/였습니다 [-at/eot/yeot-sseum-ni-da]		= (SUBJECT) VERB-ed. (polite, formal)	
VERB + -(으)ㄹ게요. [-(eu)l-kke-yo.]		= I will VERB.	

Cultural Tip

Taxi drivers in Korea are notorious for denying passengers based on their destination, especially if you try to take a taxi at night in a busy area. Some taxi drivers want to take passengers whose destination is far away, while others choose to only take passengers to a destination within a few minutes of the starting point. Nowadays, you can use a mobile app to summon a taxi by entering your current location and your destination. Sometimes, however, your request may not be accepted quickly if you try to use the app at night in a busy area.

Long Dialogue with Translation
Now challenge yourself with a longer dialogue!

택시 기사: **어디 가세요?**
Where to?

🔊 *Track 213*

수정: **경복궁이요.**
Gyeong-bok Palace.

택시 기사: **어느 쪽으로 갈까요?**
Which route shall I take?

수정: **아, 저 길 잘 몰라요.**
Oh, I don't know the routes well.

택시 기사: **성산대교는 지금 엄청 막혀요.**
Seong-san Bridge has a lot of traffic now.

수정: **그래요? 지금 늦었어요. 그래서 빨리 가야 돼요.**
Really? I'm late now. So, I have to get there quickly.

택시 기사: **그럼 양화대교로 갈게요.**
Then I'll take Yang-hwa Bridge.

수정: **네. 빨리 좀 가 주세요.**
Ok. Please hurry up.

택시 기사: **알겠습니다. 경복궁 입구로 갈까요?**
Alright. Shall I go to the entrance of Gyeong-bok Palace?

수정: **네. 입구에서 내려 주세요.**
Yes, let me out at the entrance.

택시 기사: **다 왔습니다.**
We are here.

수정: **교통 카드로 할게요.**
I will pay with a transportation card.

택시 기사: **네. 안녕히 가세요.**
Ok. Bye.

Vocabulary

어디 [eo-di]	= where	빨리 [ppal-li]	= quickly
가다 [ga-da]	= to go	그럼 [geu-reom]	= then
어느 [eo-neu]	= which	입구 [ip-kku]	= entrance
쪽 [jjok]	= side, route	내려 주다 [nae-ryeo ju-da]	= to let someone off/out
길 [gil]	= road	다 [da]	= all
잘 [jal]	= well	오다 [o-da]	= to come
모르다 [mo-reu-da]	= to not know	교통 카드 [gyo-tong ka-deu]	= transportation card
지금 [ji-geum]	= now		
엄청 [eom-cheong]	= very, so		
막히다 [ma-ki-da]	= to have a lot of traffic		
늦다 [neut-tta]	= to be late		

Grammar Points & Exercises

Study the two grammar points used in the dialogue and practice!

A. Inquiring

VERB + -시- + -아/어/여요? = Do you VERB? / Are you VERB-ing? (honorific)

* When -시- is combined with -아/어/여요, it becomes -셔요. Over time however, it changed to -세요 because it is easier to pronounce.

> **Ex)** 가다 + -시- + -아/어/여요? → 가세요? = Do you go? / Are you going?

> **1.** 오다 + -시- + -아/어/여요? ······⟩ _____
>
> = Do you come? / Are you coming?

> **2.** 보다 + -시- + -아/어/여요? ······⟩ _____
>
> = Do you watch? / Are you watching?

B. Present Perfect - Accomplishment

다 + VERB + -았/었/였습니다 = I have finished VERB-ing. / I have VERB-ed all. (polite, formal)

> **Ex)** 다 + 오다 + -았/었/였습니다 → 다 왔습니다. = I have come all the way. / We are here.

> **3.** 다 + 먹다 + -았/었/였습니다 ······⟩ _____ = I have finished eating.

4. 다 + 하다 + -았/었/였습니다 ⋯⋯⟩ _____   = I have done it all.

Track 216

Pronunciation Points & Exercises

Study the two pronunciation rules used in the dialogue and practice!

A. When a syllable ends with ㅂ and is followed by a syllable that begins with ㄱ, the ㄱ is pronounced as ㄲ.

Ex) 입구 → [입꾸]

Write the pronunciations for the following words, just like the above example.

1. 법관 (judge, the bench) ⋯⋯⟩ [   ]

2. 합격 (pass, acceptance) ⋯⋯⟩ [   ]

B. Let's review a few pronunciation rules that have been covered already.

Write the pronunciations for the following phrases from the dialogue.

3. 경복궁 ⋯⋯⟩ [   ]

4. 쪽으로 ⋯⋯⟩ [   ]

5. 막혀요 ⋯⋯⟩ [   ]

6. 늦었어요 ⋯⋯⟩ [   ]

Korean Only

Can you understand the entire dialogue without a translation? Test yourself!

- Short Dialogue

택시 기사: 다 왔습니다.

수정: 교통 카드로 할게요.

- Long Dialogue

택시 기사: 어디 가세요?

수정: 경복궁이요.

택시 기사: 어느 쪽으로 갈까요?

수정: 아, 저 길 잘 몰라요.

택시 기사: 성산대교는 지금 엄청 막혀요.

수정: 그래요? 지금 늦었어요. 그래서 빨리 가야 돼요.

택시 기사: 그럼 양화대교로 갈게요.

수정: 네. 빨리 좀 가 주세요.

택시 기사: 알겠습니다.

택시 기사: 경복궁 입구로 갈까요?

수정: 네. 입구에서 내려 주세요.

택시 기사: 다 왔습니다.

수정: 교통 카드로 할게요.

택시 기사: 네. 안녕히 가세요.

Answer Key for grammar exercises

1. 오세요? 2. 보세요? 3. 다 먹었습니다. 4. 다 했습니다.

Answer Key for pronunciation exercises

1. 법꽌 2. 합껵 3. 경복꿍 4. 쪼그로 5. 마켜요 6. 느저써요

Dialogue 37

요즘 뭐 하고 지내?
What are you up to these days?

•

Bus

Short Dialogue with Translation

Start with a simple, two-line dialogue first!

지용: **잘 지냈어? 요즘 뭐 하고 지내?**
How are you doing? What are you up to these days?

수현: **나 아직 졸업 못 했어.**
I still can't graduate.

잘
[jal]

= *well*

지내다
[ji-nae-da]

= *to live, to stay, to spend (time)*

요즘
[yo-jeum]

= *these days*

뭐
[mwo]

= *what*

하다
[ha-da]

= *to do*

나
[na]

= *I (casual)*

아직
[a-jik]

= *yet*

졸업
[jo-reop]

= *graduation*

못 VERB + -았/었/였어.
[mot   -a/eo/yeo-sseo.]

= *I couldn't VERB.*

Cultural Tip

When you take public transportation in Korea and use a transportation card, you can get a discount if you transfer between buses or between a bus and the subway within 30 minutes after you disembark. At night, you can get a discount if you transfer within one hour. Even if you have to transfer many times during your journey, it is not expensive to do so.

Long Dialogue with Translation

Now challenge yourself with a longer dialogue!

🔊 **Track 219**

지용: **어, 수현아! 오랜만이다!**
Oh, Su-hyeon. It's been a while.

수현: **어? 지용아. 진짜 오랜만이다!**
Oh? Ji-yong. It's been a really long time!

지용: **잘 지냈어? 요즘 뭐 하고 지내?**
How are you doing? What are you up to these days?

수현: **나 아직 졸업 못 했어. 지용아, 미안한데 나 버스 왔어.**
I still can't graduate. Ji-yong, I'm sorry, but my bus is coming now.

지용: **너 몇 번 타?**
What number bus do you take?

수현: **6716번.**
Number 6716.

지용: **나도 그거 타. 잘됐다. 같이 타자.**
I'm taking that, too. That's great. Let's take it together.

수현: **그래. 저기 앉자.**
Ok. Let's sit there.

지용: **너 이 버스 타고 다녀?**
Do you usually take this bus?

수현: **응. 너는 어디 가?**
Yeah. Where are you going?

지용: **나는 홍대에서 친구 만나.**
I am meeting a friend in Hongdae.

수현: **아, 이 버스 홍대 가지.**
Oh, that's right. This bus goes to Hongdae.

지용: **응. 나 이 버스 자주 타. 자주 보자.**
Yeah. I take this bus often. I'll see you often, then.

Vocabulary

오랜만이다
[o-raen-ma-ni-da]
= to have been a while

몇 번
[myeot beon]
= what number

진짜
[jin-jja]
= really

타다
[ta-da]
= to ride, to take

잘 지내다
[jal ji-nae-da]
= to be well

같이
[ga-chi]
= together

요즘
[yo-jeum]
= these days

저기
[jeo-gi]
= there

뭐
[mwo]
= what

앉다
[an-tta]
= to sit

하다
[ha-da]
= to do

어디
[eo-di]
= where

아직
[a-jik]
= yet

가다
[ga-da]
= to go

졸업
[jo-reop]
= graduation

친구
[chin-gu]
= friend

미안하다
[mi-a-na-da]
= to be sorry

만나다
[man-na-da]
= to meet

버스
[beo-sseu]
= bus

자주
[ja-ju]
= often

오다
[o-da]
= to come

보다
[bo-da]
= to see, to watch

Grammar Points & Exercises
Study the two grammar points used in the dialogue and practice!

A. Still + Present Perfect Continuous in the Negative

아직 + NOUN + 못 했어(요)
= I still have not been able to / cannot do NOUN.

Ex) 아직 + 졸업 + 못 했어(요) → 아직 졸업 못 했어(요). = I still have not been able to graduate.

1. 아직 + 결혼 + 못 했어(요)

……〉 _____ = I still can't get married.

2. 아직 + 숙제 + 못 했어(요)

……〉 _____ = I still have not been able to do homework.

B. Location/Place

NOUN + -에서 = at/in NOUN

Ex) 홍대 + -에서 → 홍대에서 = in Hongdae

3. 학교 + -에서 ……〉 _____ = at school

4. 지하철역 + -에서 ……〉 _____ = at the subway station

Study the two pronunciation rules used in the dialogue and practice!

A. When a syllable ends with ㅊ (which sounds the same as ㄷ when in the 받침 position) and is followed by a syllable that begins with ㅂ, the ㅂ is pronounced as ㅃ.

Ex) 몇 번 → [멷 번] → [멷 뻔]

Write the pronunciations for the following words, just like the above example.

    1. 꽃병 (vase) ······> [   ]

    2. 빛바래다 (to be faded) ······> [   ]

B. When a syllable ends with ㅆ (which sounds the same as ㄷ when in the 받침 position) and is followed by a syllable that begins with ㄷ, the ㄷ is pronounced as ㄸ.

Ex) 잘됐다 → [잘됃다] → [잘됃따]

Write the pronunciations for the following words, just like the above example.

    3. 있다 ······> [   ]

    4. 갔다 ······> [   ]

Korean Only

Can you understand the entire dialogue without a translation? Test yourself!

- Short Dialogue

지용: 잘 지냈어? 요즘 뭐 하고 지내?

수현: 나 아직 졸업 못 했어.

- Long Dialogue

지용: 어, 수현아! 오랜만이다!

수현: 어? 지용아. 진짜 오랜만이다!

지용: 잘 지냈어? 요즘 뭐 하고 지내?

수현: 나 아직 졸업 못 했어. 지용아, 미안한데 나 버스 왔어.

지용: 너 몇 번 타?

수현: 6716번.

지용: 나도 그거 타. 잘됐다. 같이 타자.

수현: 그래. 저기 앉자.

지용: 너 이 버스 타고 다녀?

수현: 응. 너는 어디 가?

지용: 나는 홍대에서 친구 만나.

수현: 아, 이 버스 홍대 가지.

지용: 응. 나 이 버스 자주 타. 자주 보자.

Answer Key for grammar exercises

1. 아직 결혼 못 했어(요). *2.* 아직 숙제 못 했어(요). *3.* 학교에서 *4.* 지하철역에서

Answer Key for pronunciation exercises

1. 꼳뼝 *2.* 빋빠래다 *3.* 읻따 *4.* 갇따

지하철 노선도 있어?

Do you have a subway map?

•

Subway

Short Dialogue with Translation

Start with a simple, two-line dialogue first!

 Track 223

혁: **지하철 노선도 있어?**
Do you have a subway map?

이영: **없어. 나는 거의 버스 타.**
No. I almost always take the bus.

Vocabulary

지하철 [ji-ha-cheol]	= subway
노선도 [no-seon-do]	= map
있다 [it-tta]	= to exist, to have
없다 [eop-tta]	= to not exist, to not have, to not be there
나 [na]	= I (casual)
거의 [geo-ui]	= almost
버스 [beo-sseu]	= bus
타다 [ta-da]	= to ride, to take

Cultural Tip

It is quite convenient to get around Seoul by subway. There are 21 different subway lines within and around Seoul, so more people living in satellite cities can commute to Seoul very easily. About 2 million people take Line 2, one of the busiest lines, per day.

Long Dialogue with Translation
Now challenge yourself with a longer dialogue!

이영: **집으로 가?**
Are you heading home?

🔊 **Track 225**

혁: **응. 집으로 가. 너는?**
Yeah, I'm going home. You?

이영: **나도. 너네 집 어디지?**
Me, too. Where do you live?

혁: **신촌 역. 너는 강남 역이지?**
Shinchon Station. You live near Gangnam Station, right?

이영: **응. 우리 완전히 반대편이야.**
Yeah. We live on opposite sides of the city.

혁: **그래도 같은 2호선이야.**
But we're still on the same subway line, number 2.

이영: **나 그럼 갈아타야 돼?**
Then, do I have to transfer?

혁: **시청 역까지 같이 가. 그리고 2호선으로 갈아타.**
Let's go to City Hall Station together. And [we'll] transfer to Line 2.

이영: **그렇구나. 나는 아직도 헷갈려.**
Oh, I see. I'm still confused.

혁: **진짜? 지하철 노선도 있어?**
Really? Do you have a subway map?

이영: **없어. 나는 거의 버스 타.**
No. I almost always take the bus.

혁: **그래? 지하철 노선도 앱이 있어. 그거 깔아.**
Really? There is an app for the subway map. You can install that.

이영: **그래? 알았어. 고마워.**
Really? Ok. Thanks.

Vocabulary

집 [jip]	= house, home	아직도 [a-jik-tto]	= still
가다 [ga-da]	= to go	헷갈리다 [het-kkal-li-da]	= to be confused
어디 [eo-di]	= where	지하철 [ji-ha-cheol]	= subway
완전히 [wan-jeo-ni]	= completely	노선도 [no-seon-do]	= map
반대편 [ban-dae-pyeon]	= opposite side	있다 [it-tta]	= to exist, to have
그래도 [geu-rae-do]	= but, even so	없다 [eop-tta]	= to not exist, to not have, to not be there
같다 [gat-tta]	= to be the same	거의 [geo-ui]	= almost
2호선 [i-ho-seon]	= Subway Line Number 2	버스 [beo-sseu]	= bus
갈아타다 [ga-ra-ta-da]	= to transfer	타다 [ta-da]	= to ride, to take
같이 [ga-chi]	= together	앱 [aep]	= smartphone application, app
그리고 [geu-ri-go]	= and	깔다 [kkal-da]	= to install

Grammar Points & Exercises

Study the two grammar points used in the dialogue and practice!

A. Preposition: "Toward"

NOUN + -(으)로 = toward NOUN

Track 227

Ex) 집 + -(으)로 → 집으로 = toward home

1. 반대편 + -(으)로 ······> _____ = toward the opposite side

2. 버스 정류장 + -(으)로 ······> _____ = toward the bus stop

B. Questioning an Obligation

VERB + -아/어/여야 돼(요)? = Do/Does (SUBJECT) have to VERB?

Ex) 갈아타다 + -아/어/여야 돼(요)?

  → 갈아타야 돼(요)? = Do/Does (they) have to transfer?

3. 타다 + -아/어/여야 돼(요)?

······> _____ = Do/Does (they) have to take/ride (it)?

4. 깔다 + -아/어/여야 돼(요)?

······> _____ = Do/Does (they) have to install (it)?

Study the two pronunciation rules used in the dialogue and practice!

A. When a syllable ends with ㅌ and is followed by a syllable that begins with a vowel, ㅌ becomes part of the following syllable rather than being pronounced distinctly as two different syllables.

Ex) 같은 → [가튼]

Write the pronunciations for the following words, just like the above example.

1. 붙은 ······> [   ]

2. 밭을 ······> [   ]

B. When a syllable ends with ㄱ and is followed by a syllable which begins with ㄷ, the ㄷ is pronounced as ㄸ.

Ex) 아직도 → [아직또]

Write the pronunciations for the following words, just like the above example.

3. 국도 (national highway) ······> [   ]

4. 각도 (angle) ······> [   ]

Korean Only

Can you understand the entire dialogue without a translation? Test yourself!

- Short Dialogue

혁: 지하철 노선도 있어?

이영: 없어. 나는 거의 버스 타.

- Long Dialogue

이영: 집으로 가?

혁: 응. 집으로 가. 너는?

이영: 나도. 너네 집 어디지?

혁: 신촌 역. 너는 강남 역이지?

이영: 응. 우리 완전히 반대편이야.

혁: 그래도 같은 2호선이야.

이영: 나 그럼 갈아타야 돼?

혁: 시청 역까지 같이 가. 그리고 2호선으로 갈아타.

이영: 그렇구나. 나는 아직도 헷갈려.

혁: 진짜? 지하철 노선도 있어?

이영: 없어. 나는 거의 버스 타.

혁: 그래? 지하철 노선도 앱이 있어. 그거 깔아.

이영: 그래? 알았어. 고마워.

Answer Key for grammar exercises

1. 반대편으로 2. 버스 정류장으로 3. 타야 돼(요)? 4. 깔아야 돼(요)?

Answer Key for pronunciation exercises

1. 부튼 2. 바틀 3. 국또 4. 각또

Dialogue 39

나 비행기 처음 타.

This is my first time riding an airplane.

•

Airplane

Short Dialogue with Translation

Start with a simple, two-line dialogue first!

해윤: **나 비행기 처음 타.**
This is my first time riding an airplane.

보람: **진짜? 네가 창가에 앉아.**
Really? Sit by the window.

Vocabulary

나 [na]	= I (casual)
비행기 [bi-haeng-gi]	= plane
처음 [cheo-eum]	= first time
타다 [ta-da]	= to ride, to take
진짜 [jin-jja]	= really
네 [ne]	= you (casual) * In colloquial Korean, it is often pronounced as 니 [ni] in order to avoid confusion with 내 [nae] meaning "I".
창가 [chang-kka]	= window
앉다 [an-tta]	= to sit

Cultural Tip

Prior to the Seoul Olympics in 1988, the Korean government placed many restrictions on traveling abroad, until 1989 when the restrictions were lifted and people were allowed to travel freely. Now, only Korean men over 24 who have not completed their compulsory military service have some restrictions (they have to get additional permission from the Military Manpower Administration). Many low-cost Korean airlines began operating in the late 2000s, leading to a steady increase in the number of people from Korea traveling abroad.

Long Dialogue with Translation

Now challenge yourself with a longer dialogue!

보람: **우와! 드디어 여행 시작!**
Wow! The trip finally begins!

해윤: **나 비행기 처음 타. 해외여행도 처음이야.**
This is my first time riding an airplane. It's also my first time traveling overseas.

보람: **진짜? 네가 창가에 앉아.**
Really? Sit by the window.

해윤: **그래. 기내식도 먹고 싶다.**
Ok. I want to try the in-flight meal, too.

보람: **해윤아. 우리 일본 가서 기내식 없어.**
Hae-yun, we are going to Japan, so there is no in-flight meal.

해윤: **정말?**
Really?

보람: **어. 2시간밖에 안 걸려.**
Yeah. It only takes 2 hours.

해윤: **아… 기내식 먹고 싶다.**
Argh... I want to have an in-flight meal.

보람: **해윤아, 비행기 탈 때 신발 벗고 타. 알지?**
Hae-yun, you should take off your shoes when you get in the airplane, ok?

해윤: **정말? 에이, 거짓말하지 마.**
Really? Come on, don't lie.

보람: **진짜야. 너 신발 신고 탈 거야?**
For real. Are you going to fly with your shoes on?

해윤: **거짓말하지 마. 진짜 신발 벗어?**
Don't lie. Should I really take my shoes off?

보람: **응.**
Yeah.

Vocabulary

드디어
[deu-di-eo]
= finally

먹다
[meok-tta]
= to eat

여행
[yeo-haeng]
= trip

일본
[il-bon]
= Japan

시작
[si-jak]
= start

가다
[ga-da]
= to go

비행기
[bi-haeng-gi]
= airplane

없다
[eop-tta]
= to not exist, to not have, to not be there

처음
[cheo-eum]
= first time

걸리다
[geol-li-da]
= to take (time)

타다
[ta-da]
= to ride, to take

신발
[sin-bal]
= shoes

해외여행
[hae-oe-yeo-haeng]
= traveling overseas, international trip

벗다
[beot-tta]
= to take off one's shoes

진짜
[jin-jja]
= really

거짓말하다
[geo-jin-ma-ra-da]
= to tell a lie

창가
[chang-kka]
= window

신다
[sin-tta]
= to wear, to put on one's shoes

앉다
[an-tta]
= to sit

기내식
[gi-nae-sik]
= in-flight meal

Grammar Points & Exercises
Study the two grammar points used in the dialogue and practice!

A. At the Time/When

VERB + -(으)ㄹ 때 = when (SUBJECT) VERB

Ex) 타다 + -(으)ㄹ 때 → 탈 때 = when (they) ride

1. 만나다 + -(으)ㄹ 때 ······⟩ _____ = when (they) meet

2. 먹다 + -(으)ㄹ 때 ······⟩ _____ = when (they) eat

B. Conjunction: "and"

VERB + -고 + VERB = to VERB and VERB

* The first action continues while you do the second action.

Ex) 벗다 + -고 + 타다 → 벗고 타다 = to take (it) off and ride

3. 신다 + -고 + 타다 ······⟩ _____

= to put on one's shoes and ride / to ride with one's shoes on

4. 들다 + -고 + 타다 ······⟩ _____

= to pick (it) up and ride / to ride while carrying (it)

Study the two pronunciation rules used in the dialogue and practice!

A. When a syllable ends with ㅍ (which sounds the same as ㅂ when in the 받침 position) and is followed by a syllable that begins with ㄷ, the ㄷ is pronounced as ㄸ.

Ex) 먹고 싶다　→　[먹꼬 십따]

* If you are wondering why 먹고 is pronounced as 먹꼬, please refer to page 18.

Write the pronunciations for the following words, just like the above example.

1. 깊다 (to be deep) ⋯⋯> [　　　　　　　　　　　]

2. 앞뒤 (the front and back) ⋯⋯> [　　　　　　　　　　　]

B. When a verb stem ends with ㄴ and is followed by an ending that begins with ㄱ, the ㄱ is pronounced as ㄲ.

Ex) 신고　→　[신꼬]

Write the pronunciations for the following words, just like the above example.

3. 안고 ⋯⋯> [　　　　　　　　]

4. 껴안고 ⋯⋯> [　　　　　　　　]

Korean Only

Can you understand the entire dialogue without a translation? Test yourself!

- Short Dialogue

해윤: 나 비행기 처음 타.

보람: 진짜? 네가 창가에 앉아.

- Long Dialogue

보람: 우와! 드디어 여행 시작!

해윤: 나 비행기 처음 타. 해외여행도 처음이야.

보람: 진짜? 네가 창가에 앉아.

해윤: 그래. 기내식도 먹고 싶다.

보람: 해윤아. 우리 일본 가서 기내식 없어.

해윤: 정말?

보람: 어. 2시간밖에 안 걸려.

해윤: 아… 기내식 먹고 싶다.

보람: 해윤아, 비행기 탈 때 신발 벗고 타. 알지?

해윤: 정말? 에이, 거짓말하지 마.

보람: 진짜야. 너 신발 신고 탈 거야?

해윤: 거짓말하지 마. 진짜 신발 벗어?

보람: 응.

Answer Key for grammar exercises

1. 만날 때 *2.* 먹을 때 *3.* 신고 타다 *4.* 들고 타다

Answer Key for pronunciation exercises

1. 깁따 *2.* 압뛰 *3.* 안꼬 *4.* 껴안꼬

너 자전거 탈 수 있어?

Can you ride a bicycle?

•

Bicycle

Short Dialogue with Translation
Start with a simple, two-line dialogue first!

준태: **너 자전거 탈 수 있어?**
Can you ride a bicycle?

소영: **응. 나 자전거 잘 타.**
Yeah. I ride bikes well.

Vocabulary

너 [neo]	= *you (casual)*
자전거 [ja-jeon-geo]	= *bicycle*
타다 [ta-da]	= *to ride, to take*
-(으)ㄹ 수 있다 [-(eu)l su it-tta]	= *can, to be able to*
응 [eung]	= *yes, yeah, ok (casual)*
나 [na]	= *I (casual)*
잘 [jal]	= *well*

Cultural Tip

In Korea, spring and fall are much shorter than the other two seasons, summer and winter. Additionally, because the road infrastructure in Korea is not conducive for bicycle riding, you rarely see people commute by bike. At a park however, you can see many people riding a bike for exercise or riding a tandem bike while on a date.

Long Dialogue with Translation

Now challenge yourself with a longer dialogue!

Track 237

소영: 우와! 너 자전거 샀어?
Wow! You bought a bicycle?

준태: 응. 어제 샀어. 진짜 좋아.
Yeah. I bought it yesterday. It's really good.

소영: 얼마야? 요즘 자전거 비싸지?
How much was it? Bikes are expensive these days, right?

준태: 이거는 조금 비싸. 너 자전거 탈 수 있어?
This one was a bit expensive. Can you ride a bike?

소영: 응. 나 자전거 잘 타.
Yeah. I ride bikes well.

준태: 그래? 이거 타 볼래?
Really? Do you want to try riding this?

소영: 괜찮아. 너 타.
No, thanks. You ride it.

준태: 왜? 타 봐.
Why not? Try riding it.

소영: 나 자전거 오랫동안 안 탔어. 그래서 넘어질 수도 있어. 근데 이거
얼마야?
I haven't ridden a bike in a long time. So I might fall. By the way, how
much was this?

준태: 이거? 천만 원. 진짜 좋은 거야. 타 봐.
This? It was 10 million won. It's really good. Try riding it.

소영: 뭐? 천만 원? 안 타, 안 타. 부담스러워.
What? 10 million won? I am not going to ride that.
I feel uncomfortable (with that).

Vocabulary

자전거 [ja-jeon-geo]	= bicycle	**잘** [jal]	= well
사다 [sa-da]	= to buy	**타 보다** [ta bo-da]	= to try riding
어제 [eo-je]	= yesterday	**괜찮다** [gwaen-chan-ta]	= to be ok, to be alright
진짜 [jin-jja]	= really	**오랫동안** [o-raet-ttong-an]	= for a long time
좋다 [jo-ta]	= to be good, to like	**그래서** [geu-rae-seo]	= so
얼마 [eol-ma]	= how much	**넘어지다** [neo-meo-ji-da]	= to fall
요즘 [yo-jeum]	= these days	**근데** [geun-de]	= by the way, but
비싸다 [bi-ssa-da]	= to be expensive	**얼마** [eol-ma]	= how much
이거 [i-geo]	= this, this thing	**천만 원** [cheon-man won]	= 10 million won
조금 [jo-geum]	= a little bit	**부담스럽다** [bu-dam-seu-reop-tta]	= to feel uncomfortable (doing/with something)
타다 [ta-da]	= to ride, to take		

Grammar Points & Exercises

Study the two grammar points used in the dialogue and practice!

A. Possibility

VERB/ADJECTIVE + -(으)ㄹ 수도 있다
= (SUBJECT) might VERB. / (SUBJECT) might be ADJECTIVE.

Ex) 넘어지다 + -(으)ㄹ 수도 있다 → 넘어질 수도 있다 = (They) might fall over.

1. 비싸다 + -(으)ㄹ 수도 있다 ⋯⋯⟩ _____ = (They) might be expensive.

2. 가다 + -(으)ㄹ 수도 있다 ⋯⋯⟩ _____ = (They) might go.

B. Pronoun: "something"

ADJECTIVE + -(으)ㄴ 것* = something ADJECTIVE

* 것 is often spoken as 거 because it's easier to pronounce.

Ex) 좋다 + -(으)ㄴ 것 → 좋은 것 = something good

3. 비싸다 + -(으)ㄴ 것 ⋯⋯⟩ _____ = something expensive

4. 괜찮다 + -(으)ㄴ 것 ⋯⋯⟩ _____ = something fine/ok

Study the two pronunciation rules used in the dialogue and practice!

A. Take a moment to review some pronunciation rules that were previously covered.

Write the pronunciations for the following phrases from the dialogue.

1. 탈 수 있어 ……> [   ]

2. 괜찮아 ……> [   ]

3. 오랫동안 ……> [   ]

4. 넘어질 수도 있어 ……> [   ]

5. 천만 원 ……> [   ]

6. 좋은 거야 ……> [   ]

Korean Only

Can you understand the entire dialogue without a translation? Test yourself!

- Short Dialogue

준태: 너 자전거 탈 수 있어?

소영: 응. 나 자전거 잘 타.

- Long Dialogue

소영: 우와! 너 자전거 샀어?

준태: 응. 어제 샀어. 진짜 좋아.

소영: 얼마야? 요즘 자전거 비싸지?

준태: 이거는 조금 비싸. 너 자전거 탈 수 있어?

소영: 응. 나 자전거 잘 타.

준태: 그래? 이거 타 볼래?

소영: 괜찮아. 너 타.

준태: 왜? 타 봐.

소영: 나 자전거 오랫동안 안 탔어. 그래서 넘어질 수도 있어.
　　　근데 이거 얼마야?

준태: 이거? 천만 원. 진짜 좋은 거야. 타 봐.

소영: 뭐? 천만 원? 안 타, 안 타. 부담스러워.

Answer Key for grammar exercises

1. 비쌀 수도 있다 *2.* 갈 수도 있다 *3.* 비싼 것 *4.* 괜찮은 것

Answer Key for pronunciation exercises

1. 탈 쑤 이써 *2.* 괜차나 *3.* 오랟똥안 *4.* 너머질 쑤도 이써 *5.* 천마 눤 *6.* 조은 거야

Download and listen to
the audio track at
talktomeinkorean.com/audio.